CLIFF PRESTON
CHANNELS THE ECHO

CLIFF PRESTON
CHANNELS THE ECHO

Book 2

God,
the spiritual realm,
the past and future
of humanity

Patrick Kehoe

Copyright © 2006 by Patrick Kehoe

All rights reserved under international copyright conventions.
First published in 2006 by Patrick Kehoe.

No part of this book may be reproduced or transmitted in any form or by any means, electronic or mechanical, including photocopying, recording, or by any information storage and retrieval system, without permission in writing from the author/publisher. The author and quoted sources in the book do not dispense medical advice or prescribe treatment for physical or medical problems without the advice of a physician. The purpose of this book is to offer information of a general nature. If you use any of the information in this book for yourself, the author and quoted sources assume no responsibility for your actions.

The transcripts of channeling sessions with The Echo are protected under international copyright and may not be copied in any manner without the written consent of Clifford or Linda Preston.

ISBN 978-0-9736245-1-9

Contact:
Cliff Preston   cpreston@becon.org
Patrick Kehoe   pk3@canada.com

Cover design by Patrick Kehoe

CONTENTS

Introduction

1. Cliff and Linda Preston

1. Life at sea in the Canadian navy	7
2. A channeler's view of life	18
3. It takes a psychic to know a psychic	37

2. The Echo
Original transcripts of channeling sessions for this book and other sessions — 53

4. The Echo, God, Past and Future of Humanity	55
5. The Spiritual Realm, God, Edgar Cayce	80
6. Roswell, Shag Harbour, ETs	107
7. "The Star People" by Brad Steiger	131
8. Extra-Terrestrials, Space Aliens	153

3. Appendix — 169

9. A personal channeling session with The Echo	170
10. The Echo interpret dreams	180
11. Meditation – Automatic Writing	193
12. The Echo's Code of Living and Other Statements	211
Linda Preston's essay "Science Fiction?"	216

Afterword — 218

Introduction

Cliff Preston began channeling The Echo, a group of timeless, discarnate entities, in the late 1970s to fulfill a need to help others with life's problems.

CLIFF PRESTON CHANNELS THE ECHO Book 1 (2004) introduces readers to the remarkable life and work of Cliff Preston, internationally known channeler of discarnate entities. It shows how Cliff; Linda, his wife and trance director; and The Echo, a nearly uncountable group of spirits, started on a course which brings spiritual wisdom to life's problems.

The first part of the book describes Cliff's difficult life-long personal search for answers to his questions about life and his place in it. It explains his breakthrough with Spirit which has helped thousands of persons who have had contact with him. There is also a moving look into a man's soul as he struggles to help his dying wife recover from illness. This chapter from Cliff's personal diary details Linda's miraculous recovery from encephalitis, after doctors had given up hope. Cliff's own courageous words credit her recovery to the constant attention of alternative practitioners.

The second part of the book presents several exclusive transcripts of Cliff's deep-trance channeling sessions of The Echo. There are two sessions in the presence of the Mitchell-Hedges Crystal Skull, believed to be a 100,000-year-old interplanetary communication device. Other subjects include spirituality, psychism for beginners, meditation and relaxation, imagination - creating your reality, and alcoholism.

Book 2 (2006) portrays the dangers of Cliff's life at sea, more psychic experiences of Canada's ordinary extraordinary psychic couple in many parts of North America, the relationship between Cliff, Linda, and The Echo, and their view of life. There are more transcripts of Cliff's deep-trance channeling sessions of The Echo on such subjects as The Echo, God, the past and future of humanity, and personal dream interpretation.

Book 3 (2008) reveals underwater recovery diving in Cliff's reminiscences, more about their view of life, and more psychic experiences such as Linda's encounter with Jesus. There are more transcripts of Cliff's deep-trance channeling sessions of The Echo on such subjects as messages from The Echo, Jesus Christ, Extra-Terrestrials and other mysteries.

I heard about Cliff when I was looking for a trance channeler in the style of Edgar Cayce. Seeing him channel The Echo was fascinating. He maintained a trance with a new persona and voice for one hour and 29 minutes, never opening his eyes or losing the mood. His body moved only if his trance director requested the new persona move it for him. The channeled answers to my questions carried the essence of truth and went beyond what I had expected. A new world opened.

A short time later, I attended a psychic information and meditation evening. Each guest gave a brief personal introduction. I said that I am a writer and perhaps I will write a book about Cliff Preston and The Echo some day. I said it with some hope, but no conviction.

As I was writing the first book in June, 2004, I asked The Echo during one channeling session, how I had received the definite idea to write and publish a book, a few years after that psychic evening.

The Echo replied:

"This be gentle nudge by we. We wish the informations that be available here to be made known to, that refer, general public. The form of the one Clifford originally wrote its adventures for the purpose of informing its sons about its life as it find estrangement with sons. However, we wish this be carried an step or two further and allow these informations be shared with all."

I consider Cliff and The Echo my co-authors. They had the idea of a book first. Cliff readily agreed to work together. He provided what he had written previously - the section from his personal diary and passages for what he thought could be an autobiography some day. He provided selected written transcripts of his deep-trance channeling sessions of The Echo. Cliff and Linda answered my questions and approved my suggestions, writing, rewriting, editing, and cover design.

Chapter 1   Life at sea in the Canadian navy

Another storm during a dark, cold November night on the North Atlantic Ocean. The Canadian navy destroyer HMCS Algonquin was in serious trouble.

The ship had never reacted this badly during a storm before. Normally, a helmsman can maneuver a ship to meet the oncoming waves so that the whole ship will rise to ride the crest of a wave and set down in the trough before the next wave. Most of the force and the water pass along the underside of the ship. The powerful, towering waves are mostly repetitive and predictable. The strong wind is constant and mostly from one direction. The ship can find its groove and stay in it. This was the accepted way to manage a ship during a storm at sea.

However this time, the winds were gusting from different directions. They were random and unpredictable. This created choppiness in the water. As the ship's bow ploughed into a wave, the ship shuddered left and right as chop hit it on all sides, pushing it around like a corkscrew. There was no pattern, and no trough to settle in before riding the next wave.

The frantic helmsman had almost lost control. It seemed impossible to position the ship to miss or minimize any of the fury. Every minute or two, he desperately set and reset course. First one way, then the other. Starboard, then port, then starboard again. It was futile. The destroyer took the full force of the wind and the full force of every wave.

The raging ocean was toying with the ship. As the fierce winds blasted the ship from different directions, the angry 50-foot waves crashed repeatedly over the bow, flooding the decks and washing backwards. The two lookouts over the bridge and the watchman at the stern clung to their posts. As the ship rocked and threw them off balance, the constant need to recover their footing drained their energy.

Able-bodied seaman Cliff Preston was called to the bridge that night to read the roll indicator. He had been in his quarters after his shift on deck had ended in the afternoon. As armourer's mate he was responsible for explosives. He was not usually required to stand watches.

It was wild in the bridge and on the deck. The majority of the crew below deck could not have had any idea how bad it was over their heads.

He looked at the roll indicator. It measured in incremental units, from zero, in the middle, to 36° on the port side and 36° on the starboard side, left and right. He knew this meant that the ship was designed to stay afloat only up to a 36° angle on either side. The captain had to know when the ship was close to rollover so he could give the order to the helmsman to turn hard port or hard starboard. The order would be for only a few seconds. It would be an extreme measure necessary to keep the ship from sinking. Cliff began to shout aloud the readings when the roll indicator reached 25° on either side. The two danger zones.

"Twenty-five. Twenty-six. Twenty-seven. Twenty-nine. Thirty. Thirty-two. Thirty-three."

The 21-year-old was terrified. He sensed the fear around him in the bridge, although the helmsman and the three or four officers tried not to show it. The storm had the ship and the crew of 170 at its mercy. Everyone's life depended on fewer than half a dozen men

"Thirty-two. Thirty-three."

If the ship went down, there would be no chance of anyone being rescued, far off the eastern coast of Newfoundland. The few, exhausted men on deck would be flung into the sea. The majority would be trapped inside the ship as she turned over and sank. The bridge crew would be among those trapped. But he knew that at least they would have done everything they could. Or anyone else could.

"Thirty-three. Thirty-four."

His wife was home in Halifax. They had been married earlier that year. They had just started their life together. At least she would be safe.

"Thirty-three. Thirty-four."

His mother, Hazel, was in Aurora, a town north of Toronto. She had spent her whole life in the same area. Smart. She would be safe too.

"Thirty-three. Thirty-two."

God let us live. A Canadian navy destroyer can not sink in a storm. We will be okay, he told himself.

"Thirty-three. Thirty-four."

His sister Fern was also home in Ontario. She and her family would be safe too.

"Thirty-five."

The ship really is going to sink. He could see that the waves were still coming at odd angles. They were unpredictable. No wonder the helmsman could not seem to set the ship to meet the waves.

"Thirty-four."

Two hours had gone by.

He thought of his father. His father had died when Cliff was seven. His father had worked, drank, and gambled, never having had much time for his son. Cliff had only a few memories of his father. He had joined the navy at age 18, partly because of problems with his step-father and partly because of problems at school. He was also driven to find the answers to his many questions about life. Now, he may find some of the answers only by losing his own life. Or maybe there would be no answers at all.

"Thirty-five."

The men in the bridge seemed to be coming to terms with the danger. They were still afraid but it did not seem to matter as much. They were all doing their jobs. They knew this could happen when they signed on. They were well-trained. They were not showing their panic.

"Thirty-four."

He was tiring from his long day and night. His full day-shift and now this desperate struggle. Call it the graveyard shift. That name seemed appropriate. If only the sailors did not have to keep finding their footing. Just when he was set, he was thrown off balance again and again. As was everyone else.

Three hours had now gone by. He was getting too tired to think any more. He did not know what the others thought. Probably better that most of the men did not know what was going to happen to them.

"Thirty-five."

His numbed mind leaped back and forth. Repeating the same thoughts. The same feelings. They could not possibly get out of this. Just one more wave breaking over the ship could send them down. No, they would be fine. They had survived everything the storm could throw at them for hours. It could not possibly get any worse. Fear. Resignation. Hope. Back and forth. The ordeal lasted six hours.

Cliff says that it had been a rough night, but by morning everything quickly returned to normal. Every sailor became a weatherman because sailors lived with the weather every day and had to learn how to meet any kind of weather conditions. However, the crew took that kind of thing in stride. When they signed on in the navy, they knew storms were a possibility. They never thought about storms until they were in one. Then, after the storm was behind them, they were no longer concerned about it. Perhaps it was their military training. Perhaps the invincible feeling of youth. Or some trust in something even greater and vaster than the ocean. Even if they were frightened sometimes, they would never want to show it. The men talked about the storm for a while, but they went about their normal duties.

"We saw it as sometimes the sea acts up and we, as human beings, are always at the mercy of the elements. We took what came along and worked with it. The minute the sea went back to a manageable state, the storms were forgotten."

The officers noted the specifics of the storm for the record. However, there were no special suggestions about how to avoid such storms or how to deal with bad weather in the future.

Hurricane Diane in August, 1955, had been a worse storm overall, but did not present as much danger. The HMCS Iroquois was between Halifax, Nova Scotia, and Bermuda when the storm struck. At great cost, the crew of the ship battled the hurricane for almost five days but had always expected that they could maintain control of their ship. Seas crested at between 80 feet and 90 feet, tearing off all the fittings from the upper deck, boat davits, and guard rails from the sides of the ship. Day after day, the ship rocked constantly. Seasickness overcame most of the crew. They took short intervals of sleep whenever possible. Fifteen, twenty minutes here and there. It was mostly a concern for the men who were still functioning. For the rest it was not as important how much sleep they had. At the end, only Cliff, four other seamen and one officer were still on their feet out of a similar crew to the Algonquin of approximately 170. Two crewmen in the radar room had kept at work, despite their seasickness, with buckets at their feet. The rest were too seasick to be of any help.

"Most of these sailors would never have been seasick, but the intensity and duration of the storm overcame them. Seasickness throws off the balancing mechanism in the inner ear. When their sense of balance has been lost, they can not do much until after they have recovered.
"Things are different in the navy today, especially with better weather reporting, but that was the 1950s," Cliff says calmly.

Sailors were taught some basic swimming and survival techniques in the water, but the men went to sea never expecting to be thrown overboard or to have their ship sink. Consequently, many of the sailors could not swim properly. On one occasion, when the ship was a day out of Halifax, in the warm water of the Gulf Stream, the crew stopped for some recreation. They threw a net over the side of the ship, forming a safe area to swim, clear of the ship. Some of the men ran to the side and jumped into the impromptu swimming pool. Cliff jumped into the ocean but missed the net. The surge of the waves carried him farther and farther away. His dog-paddle was inadequate to get him back to the ship. A couple of sailors swam out and escorted him back.

"With all the confusion and the shouting, I heard a gunshot. When I got back to the net and I was climbing up the side of the ship, the officer of the watch told me to take a look out there. So I looked back and I saw a six-foot shark floating belly up. They had shot it from the deck of the ship. They told me I had almost been dinner for the shark."

This made such an impression on him that after the ship was back in port at the Halifax naval base, he went to the swimming pool every day for two or three months. He swam and swam. Approximately six weeks after the episode with the shark, he won his section of a swimming meet, including all the ships and land bases in the area.

"All I could think of was the shark on my tail."

Becoming a good swimmer would later help him realize his childhood dream of becoming a scuba diver. On a few occasions before he took formal training to gain accreditation in this new skill, he put on scuba gear, and went below the surface of the water, with some experienced navy divers. He was in the Caribbean Islands. A wonderful place to start scuba diving. After leaving the navy, he moved back to Ontario. Shortly after moving to Fort Erie, on the Canadian side of the Niagara River from Buffalo, New York, Cliff trained with the volunteer Fort Erie Underwater Recovery Team, a new unit within the fire department. After completing his specialized training, he was accepted as a volunteer recovery diver of drowning victims. He would be in the water often six days a week for the next 10 years, doing something he loved, and helping ease the pain of families and friends of drowning victims.

Scuba diving surpassed his two great youthful interests of running and being in the woods, alone with nature and his own thoughts. It became a spiritual retreat for Cliff as an adult. Scuba diving became his life. It was a form of self expression and an opportunity to help others. He loved to dive and to teach others to dive. Diving also provided a sanctuary from his troubled first marriage or any other problem.

"Diving became the closest thing to real spirituality and a way of being with God. Beneath the surface of the waters, there is a freedom of movement and a sense of oneness with one's own great spirit. The soaring above the rocks and the coasting on invisible currents that sweep one along, create a new perspective and a new way of learning.

"I believe it teaches personal spiritual satisfaction. Many times in my life, when things seemed difficult or hopeless, I would submerge my body and soul beneath the healing waters. There I was free. I could move with the ease of thought. I was in control."

Yet two omens would end his scuba diving.

The first disturbing experience led to the end of Cliff's association with the diving recovery team.

"While answering an emergency call, I was driving my car to the recovery unit building to gather my diving equipment. Somehow, some powerful force kept me driving past the building. Some thing or some strong impression influenced me so overwhelmingly that I returned to my home and did not dive at all that day. The sensation of impending doom was so intense that I stopped diving for the recovery team soon after."

For several years after this experience, he took part only in occasional outings with a few trusted friends as diving partners.

Many years later, working for the government of the Northwest Territories, he acted as government liaison for a project in which commercial divers inspected underwater piping extending a mile from shore under the sea. This exhilarating experience of observing the young divers and recording the operation, gave Cliff an idea. He could use all his years of diving experience again by passing on his knowledge to other young divers. He registered for a diving instructor training program in the Florida Keys, held during his vacation, on the other side of the continent.

The first day of training was spent in review work, practicing basic pool skills and getting to know the other instructors and the students. Each participant was pool-tested to be sure that he was physically fit and qualified to continue safely with the training. They would be taken to an ocean reef the next day.

Cliff was elated. He would be diving on a coral reef for the first time since his navy days, 30 years ago. This was wonderful.

But then the dream came.

In his dream, he saw the diving boat, near the reef, tossing wildly on an angry sea. He saw frantic activity among the persons on board. There was a sense of panic. Dark clouds raced overhead, obliterating the sun. Wind and rain lashed the tiny vessel, yet there was no move to run before the storm. Everyone was peering over the side in awed expectation. The heads of divers popped through the surface of the water. They were carefully holding something.

The dream scene shifted to a better view of the object that the divers were holding.

They were holding Cliff.

He was lifeless. His face had the familiar blue tinge of drowning victims.

Cliff had drowned. He was the object of a recovery search. He was dead.

He awakened with a fearful start and realized that he was standing in the middle of the hotel room floor.

It was only a dream. Thank God.

The dream was so upsetting that Cliff cancelled his training in the morning. He has never dived since that horrible dream.

He knows that he could have toughed it out and completed the course. He knows that he could have been "macho."

He also knows that later that same morning, the Florida Keys were suddenly and unexpectedly struck by a hurricane that lasted for the next two days. All boats in the area were ordered to the safety of port.

In retrospect, Cliff says that "going to sea was one of the best things I ever did. People tend to be more sure of themselves after they have been at sea. We learned about life and possible death. We thought about our own mortality. At any second, the sea could swallow you whole. It gives people a new definition of who they are and where they fit in the world.

"On an ocean you are not bombing around the way you may be on a lake. The ocean is always in control. It can make you feel very small. There is nowhere to run. If you find yourself in trouble, you have to find a way out of it. In the case of a large ship, you learn that if you don't work together, none of you will survive. It is always necessary to work together. So you learn responsibility for yourself and for others. We knew that after any kind of incident, the sea would just roll on as if nothing had happened."

At the time, had the young sailor been running away from his problems by going to sea? Would he find the answers about life that he had been seeking for most of his short existence? Perhaps he was following a pre-ordained route that would lead him to his life's purpose.

A puzzling clue awaited him in San Juan, Puerto Rico, where shore leave, on this occasion, turned into a bar fight. Terrified at seeing knives and hearing shouts of "Kill him"; Cliff ran out into the street. Five angry men chased the former high school runner, as he ran the most important race of his life through the dark and deserted streets of the old city. But he could not lose his pursuers. In desperation, he turned into a covered alley about as long as a city-block. Catching his breath half-way in, he glanced back and glimpsed several forms.

He turned forward to continue running as a tiny, brilliant light appeared in the darkness ahead. Cliff froze. The light grew larger and brighter. It took the shape of a man's head and the features of a face ? his father's face. It hovered slightly above eye level and smiled at Cliff. In a clear, distinct voice the face said, "Don't worry." It shrank to a tiny sparkle of light and disappeared. The episode took only a second or two, time that Cliff did not have. Tensing for action, he looked back again at his pursuers. They had vanished. Cliff was alone in the dark and silent alley. His fear had gone too. He cautiously made his way back to his ship without incident.

"I always had a kind of belief in the psychic since that incident in San Juan, Puerto Rico, when my deceased father's face flashed in front of me as a sign of encouragement. I was 21 or 22. I was not hallucinating. That was the real thing. However, for a number of years, I still thought the psychics at fairs were frauds and weird people," Cliff says.

As the first book was being written, The Echo replied to a question about what gave Cliff the determination to learn channeling. The reply included the following comment on the incident in San Juan. It indicates a spiritual calling.

"This also be a degree of push from we. As we be, prior stated, waiting in the wings. We offer to this entity a beginning point in that of the year 1958-59 by allowing the entity to view the face of its male parent while the entity be in danger and the danger vanishing. This be done in order to assist the entity in opening. However, the entity be of stubborn format and require a degree of time in the life of the entity."

This was one of the first of many psychic experiences in Cliff's life, and perhaps the most memorable. He would certainly pay attention to such incidents, wonder about them, and continue his restless search for answers, which traditional sources did not seem able to provide. In time, he became more comfortable with these inexplicable events. He was able to form some theories about them, based on reading and talking to other persons who had a similar interest. However, there were many other concerns in his life. There was day-to-day living with its myriad demands, distractions and problems. There was a lack of a belief system, or context, that would accept and explain all the unusual things that intrigued him. Even his own dismissal of psychic practitioners, from his lack of knowledge of them, while accepting the psychic, might have delayed his opening to Spirit and his own psychic development. He would not dedicate himself to psychic things or spirituality for many more years. Still, whether or not he was aware of it, his conscious interest in the psychic and his desire to help others were moving him closer, through the years, to his life purpose. He came to realize that his life purpose is to help others, mainly as a channeler.

Chapter 2   A channeler's view of life

The term "Original Age" describes this book better than the term "New Age", because the first term suggests an understanding of life and of our world which has existed as long as the human spirit. Sometimes this awareness has been obscured, but it can never be lost, because it is part of us.

This understanding of life says that human beings are eternal spirits who reside in the timeless present of a spiritual realm. They grow spiritually in that realm through such things as love, acts of kindness, study and achievement. The purpose of this growth is to become closer to God. They may choose to grow spiritually at a faster pace by dealing with circumstances and difficulties not available in this ideal spiritual world. For this type of growth, it is necessary for them to enter bodies in a physical world and temporarily lose conscious memory of their previous existence. Our physical world is a classroom and a proving ground, where we learn certain lessons and overcome certain problems. We are more alive as spirits in our own realm than we are as physical beings in this realm, with diminished senses and limited awareness.

From the perspective of our physical world, the proof of our human reality has always been elusive. We assume that there is a common, objective, external reality, which we all experience in the same way. We assume that this can be proven by science and, in some cases, by as little as two persons agreeing that something is true or that an event happened as they recall it. However, we do not all view the world in the same way, see the same things, or experience the same things. Witnesses in court sometimes disagree. The things we remembered clearly last week may now be beyond our conscious recollection. Do we, as individuals, even understand what we experience in our own lives? Perhaps the endless repetition of our daily routines puts us in a trance. Our lives may be on automatic pilot because we let our own assumptions guide us, or we accept what others have told us about the world, rather than looking closely at things to determine their true nature for ourselves. We talk about "sleepwalking through life". Sometimes we joke that we may all be characters in someone else's dream.

Perhaps we experience reality when we sleep and dream. Many dreamers have a feeling or conviction that some aspects of the dream are more real in some way than their waking reality. Sometimes, as we return to the dream state, we seem to remember truths that are hidden during waking hours. We instantly affirm during the dream: "I know that. I must have forgotten it somehow. Yes, I know that is true." In our dreams, we can float in the air over housetops because we seem to be presences or intelligences rather than physical bodies. We can communicate by telepathy. We can consciously will certain things to happen and other things not to happen. It would be wonderful to have these abilities during our waking hours. Perhaps we do.

Individuals who have had near-death experiences, say that they visited a reality that is much greater than ours. They say that while in this altered state of consciousness, they remembered universal truths which they had forgotten in their daily lives. Feelings and sensations are intensified. Colors are more radiant. Beautiful music pulses with the rhythm of creation. Upon returning to this existence, they once again forgot some of these truths, available only in a higher consciousness. Their senses, once again, became desensitized as life seemed to become slower and less vibrant. Their experiences, such as reading the printed information on the top of the blades of a fan attached to the ceiling, as they seemed to hover and look down at the occupants of the room, exceed the simulation in a laboratory of some reported sensations.

Some think that we experience reality after consuming alcohol or other drugs and feeling the first pleasant sensation of an expansion of consciousness, perception, creativity, love or connection. Our certainty of this reality increases with consumption. However, our certainty and our experience of this reality usually disappear with sobriety. Surely it was "just the alcohol talking" or, in this case, the alcohol thinking, or not thinking. Yet, what if this state, too, is a form of reality, normally unavailable to us? Even some religious ritual is based on the achievement of altered states of awareness.

Quantum physics shows that everything in the physical world that appears as a solid object is actually a wave or vibration of energy. Matter is not solid. The tiniest subatomic particles, which could be expected to be the building blocks of actual, undeniable, physical reality, seem to be something completely different. These fickle particles seem to be waiting to draw their definition and animation from outside themselves. They exist as possibilities, many different possibilities at once, and not as definite objects. Even the space between these particles, which should be empty, is not. It is here that the meaning of our universe probably lies - the Zero Point Field. This is the energy source for the particles. They are indivisible from it and are in constant interaction with it, absorbing their energy and other information from it. Also, they Rather than proving the separation and isolation of all things, scientific investigation has shown the interconnectedness and continuity of all things.

The fact that we see things as solid matter, many believe, is just a shared conscious illusion. Our subconscious minds are part of a unified awareness and purpose which determine the nature of our conscious reality. In effect, our subconscious minds are the projectors and our conscious minds are the viewing screens. We agree to watch the same movie as we begin life, but we choose different seats in the theatre, pay varying degrees of attention to what we see, and form different opinions of what we have seen. Those who become aware that we can choose our own movie, in effect, leave the theatre, go home and run their own movies. They consciously tell their subconscious minds what they are going to experience. This will happen, many say, if we have the determination to direct our subconscious and create our own reality.

Quantum physics also shows that the observer can change objects and events merely by the acts of observation or thought.

The uncertain subatomic particles become certain when they are observed, measured, or analyzed.

Other types of scientific investigation have shown that human beings can affect the outcome of experiments by consciously willing certain results. It has also been shown that human beings can communicate telepathically.

In our day-to-day world, a tree falling in the forest creates only energy waves. It is unorganized information. It takes an observing intelligence to organize this information into an apparent object called a tree, apparently falling and striking the ground, or striking another object and making a noise. A different observing intelligence may organize the available information differently, so that it sees and experiences the event differently.

Individuals and groups are credited with incidents of healing without medical intervention by sending concentrated thoughts and specific visualizations of health, or by general prayer that someone return to health. This suggests that the conscious can direct the subconscious and that the subconscious can accept direction from the conscious. The amazing implication is that we can create our own reality. We can direct ideas to take form.

If the external world is a temporary illusion, as spirituality, and also some areas of science suggest, where does that leave us? With the understanding that the way to truth, the way to self-discovery and the way to God are within us. Ultimately, these are the same thing. By opening our minds and listening to our inner silence, we will discover who we are, our purpose, and our link with the divine. This is one name for the source of all life, the ultimate purpose, the order and intelligence in the universe.

Is the Zero Point Field the mind of God? As part of this universal field of interconnection, are we able to think like God and co-create our realities with God?

***

Cliff sees the purpose and consistency in his own life.

"Everything in my life has happened for a reason. Overall, I think the reason was to get me to the point where I could be a channeler. I think part of the reason that my father died when I was seven, was so that I would learn to stand on my own two feet. I think the reason I stammered until about age 40 was so that I would learn how it felt. I would learn what compassion means to people. There were times when I experienced compassion being directed to me, and there were times when I had to direct compassion to other people. I had to learn both sides of it.

"All the experiences that I have undergone have taught me something that has really helped me in dealing with people in channeling. Over almost 30 years, I have dealt with people in every walk of life, through Echo sessions for all manner of reasons. This includes the wife of a member of parliament, a prime minister's pilot, housewives, children dying of illnesses.

"It seems like only yesterday when I was a child, 10 or 11, hunting groundhogs. However, my first marriage seems as if it was on another planet, or a different life. When that phase of my life ended and I took all the things I had learned from it, I think my life got back on track again. It moved in the direction that I needed to go."

*

What does he think is the importance of channeling?

"I would say that it helps to create peace of mind for clients. We have often encountered people who were emotionally troubled or suffering from guilt complexes, things like that, which were usually related to their families or their spouses. Receiving channeled information eases those difficulties. It helps people deal with that kind of thing and other things such as accidents or job losses.

"Generally a channeling session gives people a sense of peace. They understand that they are not always alone or always wrong. There is always an opportunity to change things. It gives people the ability to understand that they can change things in their own lives. It provides people with a broader outlook on life.

"We have encountered in channeling many individuals who are afraid to make a move in any direction in their lives because it doesn't meet the accepted rules and regulations they have grown up with. It doesn't meet what they think the great "they" out there expect of them. The truth is that no one else cares. When teenagers go to a school dance and then stand around outside of the dance floor, they worry that everyone else is going to see them and think that they look stupid on the dance floor. However, when they get out on the dance floor, nobody else cares.

"Channeling can help people to understand there is more to life than imposed rules and regulations and the supposedly imposed social mores. In our society it is necessary to have some social regulations or people would be living in anarchy. I think that it is important that people understand the difference between necessary rules and unnecessary rules or arbitrary requirements. Guilt trips are rampant especially among partners. Many are constantly laying blame for things in their lives on each other. Their homes are no longer places of solace but places of conflict.

"We used to do some counseling with couples. I asked them why they would take out their day's anger on the person they professed to love. They would ask who else was there? I said why not deal with the persons who made you angry? When you go home it has to be your place of solace from the outside world. It makes no sense to bring the anger home and dump it on your partner.

"Ideally, channeling helps clients come to rely on themselves and to trust their own inner voices or intuition. They will learn what is best for themselves. Their direction should come from within, not from suppositions, assumptions, arbitrary ideas, or a misplaced sense of obligation.

"I have learned through channeling and through other experiences in my life, that life is, or can be, simpler and less difficult than we make it. It starts with the fact that everyone is responsible for himself. An individual may have some responsibilities to other persons in his life, in that he is accountable for how he treats them. However, he has no responsibilities for those other persons. He is not accountable for the decisions they make, or the things they do. They are responsible for themselves. No one has the right to impose rules or conditions on another person, beyond the normal conditions of that relationship, such as parent-child, partners, or employer-employee.

"The meaning of life is spiritual, not materialistic. Consider others often, not just ourselves. It is better to share what we have with others, rather than trying to hoard everything for ourselves.

"I think there is a monstrous difference between the reality of human existence and the social mores around us. Our society is based on rules and regulations. The human animal grows up without rules and regulations in the reality of existence. If we lived in the forest like natives, there would be no unnecessary rules and regulations. We would grow up without fears and phobias."

*

Does he think channeling is special?

"I think that channeling is ordinary. Almost anyone who has the interest could learn to do it. I do not think of my channeling as amazing. That doesn't make good reading in the book, but I can say that I think the human mind is an amazing, wonderful thing. Everything comes from the mind.

"The ability to connect with a higher level has always been part of mankind. I believe that spiritual direction has been channeled and that some religious scriptures have been channeled. This may be another way of saying that the information comes through intuition or that it is God speaking.

"Another point is not to be exclusive. Consider the validity of the information and the applicability to your life. We have run into some people in channeling who would say that another channeler is wrong because the information they received is right. Perhaps there is a misunderstanding. Perhaps they are talking about different things.

"What some people may consider unusual events, I think, are quite common. There is a connection between the minds of human beings and the minds of those we say are departed, but in fact, are near us in another dimension."

He gives the example of an ex-wife's house. She remarried almost immediately after divorcing Cliff, assuming custody of their sons. Six months later, her new husband died. Cliff sometimes helped by babysitting their sons when she was working. Cliff purchased a toy cowboy made of beads with a battery in the bottom compartment. Cords that were under tension, became slack when a wheel turned. In a full cycle, the toy cowboy fell over and stood up again.

"A couple of times, I heard a clatter in the bedroom but the boys were sleeping. I thought I would remove the battery to keep the toy from working and making a noise. After I picked it up, I noticed that there was no battery in it."

Cliff thought it was just the former husband saying that he was all right.

"On another occasion, the light in the bathroom came on and off three or four times. Okay, I thought, I get the idea."

It was also not a surprise to Cliff when his ex-wife phoned to say that all the taps were running when she came home in the afternoons. He went over to the house and told her that her ex-husband was letting her know that he was there. It was nothing to be alarmed about.

"I think these are common experiences, but people tend to 'logic' them away. If you ask them three days later, they will say the events never happened."

A friend also had experiences after the death of a loved one, in which lights and water turned on and off. Knocking was heard at the door when no one was there.

*

Since Cliff accepted psychic experiences from early adulthood, has he attracted such things more than someone else, such as an atheist would?

"Some people have closed their minds to unusual things. We see only things that our minds are open enough to see. The classic case is the Spanish coming to North America. We are told that the natives could not see their ships because they had no frame of reference to understand what the ships were. A medicine man had to study the horizon regularly, before he could see the ships. Next, he had to tell the others what he had seen, before they could see it too.

"I think psychic knowledge is normal and natural. We have not delved deeply enough into it. We will not learn more about it by denying it or ignoring it. However, I don't think scientific investigation into the mind with probes will ever prove anything. Psychic awareness can not be forced or reduced to fit a theory."

*

If someone considers things to be ordinary, that many others consider as extraordinary, how does he maintain his sense of awe and wonder about life? How does he become enthusiastic about things? Has he never sat back and thought "wow" he can channel?

"A sense of wonder is natural to me. I have always been interested in why and how things happen. I have never sat back and thought, 'Wow, I am a channeler.' I just had a drive to do it. Although, I did sit back and wonder how did being a stationary engineer fit in with channeling? Those two things are at opposite ends of the same spectrum."

*

If he thinks channeling is ordinary, why was he determined to learn how to do it after he observed his first channeling session?

"Unconsciously that session triggered in me the awareness that channeling is a way to make a difference and to help other people. I think my entire life purpose is to channel and to be helping people in any way I can. That came out in me in the navy. Anytime someone got hurt, he came to me to bandage him.

Then I sent the person to the ship's sick bay. People also came to me with their problems when I was a supervisor in a factory."

His sense of fair play was evident when he worked in Buffalo, New York, as a shift-supervisor at Bernel Foam Company, a manufacturer of polyurethane foam for the furniture and automotive industries.

The year was about 1970. There was a posting for a tow motor operator. He gave the position to a female employee applicant, whom he believed had the physical strength to do the work. In the office, he was told that he could not give the position to a female employee. He was instructed to tell her that she could not have the job. So he informed her what he had been told. Then he suggested that she seek assistance from her union. She took the problem to her union. There was a legal challenge. Her side won the challenge and the woman was given the job. This was one of the first equal rights cases in New York State at that time.

"I have never believed in kicking people when they are down. I wanted to help them. I suppose other persons sensed this about me. It was the same thing when I joined the underwater recovery team. My purpose was to ease the pain of people who are losing family members. It was a secondary thing that I learned more about diving. It was a rewarding experience for me to dive with that group of men.

"When channeling came up, it seemed that my life path opened up before me. I would no longer be going to work every day and going home every night, with little sense of accomplishment, just to make someone else rich. There was a great deal of satisfaction for me to see that I could help people in a meaningful way. I also realized that I could answer a need in myself that had been there all my life."

*

Does commercialism affect psychic ability?

"I do not think a psychic's power will fail if he values money over more important things. I think a person's psychic abilities will remain but, somewhere along the line, he will run into blocks that he can't overcome because he has created them for himself.

"I believe that Karma happens in this life. If someone becomes negative or does negative things, he is creating a kind of Karma, with blocks which may be difficult or impossible to overcome. If you go after the psychic field to make big money, it does not work. Because in order to make big money you enter negative thought programming. Positive thought programming does not make big money in the spiritual field."

*

What is a client's best preparation for a channeling session?

"We usually recommend that a scheduled client write a series of questions and edit the questions every day before attending the session. A client will find that, sometimes, answers will come to him just by thinking about the questions and revising the list.

"When clients do not have their questions written down, they may not be able to remember all their questions. After a session they say, 'I should have asked such and such'. The second time they may decide to write their questions.

"When they listen to the cassette tape that we provide, they realize that the session is not completely the same as what they thought they remembered. The Echo speak in a particular manner and it does not take too much to change the meaning. Minds tend to hear what they think they should hear. We recommend that everyone make a list of questions, if possible, and listen to the tape after the session."

*

Does Cliff have the answers he has been seeking all his life?

"Maybe I have some answers that I have been looking for. I do not think I will ever have all the answers I have wanted."

He does not think that giving Linda a list of questions to ask while he is channeling is the best way for him.

"I have to go through things and experience things for myself. I have learned a lot through channeling, but my real purpose in channeling is to help others."

Friends and clients sometimes comment that Cliff misses the information that he channels, as he usually has no conscious recollection of any part of a channeling session.

"Yes, I suppose that I have been sound asleep for 30 years. I am actually 120 years old. Just well rested," he says with a laugh.

Cliff says his only questions, which he had someone else ask for him, were about the incident when his father's face appeared before him and about other psychic phenomena such as occurrences when his sons were small. He seldom felt the need to ask for direction from another source.

"A lot of people do feel the need to ask direction from another source. So we help them with that. However, The Echo never tell anybody they have to do anything. The idea is that the information they receive can help people start to rely on themselves and get back on their spiritual paths."

*

How does he see life?

"I think that everyone is here in this life to learn something, whether negative things or positive things.

"If human beings co-operated there would be no starvation or killing others because of greed for land, money, or power. It is not a perfect world. There are a number of people who believe their only purpose for being here is to get, gather, or build things for themselves.

"I remember a bumper sticker on a car reading in big letters: *He who has all the toys, still dies.*

"So what is the point of trying to get all the toys for yourself? People who are strictly materialistic lose their real sense of themselves. In the channeling, we have encountered some extremely materialistic persons. They could not even understand the spiritual things The Echo related to their lives. When the session was over they would say: "Why are they talking about that, when all I wanted to know about was my money?"

*

The Western mind may have difficulty understanding the growing phenomenon of healing by third party, with or without medical intervention. Yet millions of persons of all faiths regularly pray for the sick. Studies have shown that persons who are prayed for can have a better recovery rate than those in similar circumstances receiving no prayer. Some cures are considered miraculous, happening after human science dictates that they can not happen. Healing has long been a tradition in many cultures around the world. Cliff learned healing from exercises in his first courses about psychic development and mind training.

"There are two things to remember in healing. First, the human mind is much more powerful than we normally give it credit for. Second, we are connected to everything in the universe. If you know this, helping someone else heal is not that big a deal. You make a mental and emotional connection and visualize the other person as whole and healthy.

"You can help someone that you have never met, even at a distance. I suppose that I, and Linda, together and alone, have sent healings thousands of times. All it takes is a thought. It will either be accepted or not accepted by the intended recipient. There have been many beneficial results.

"Over the years we have learned that there is only one healer. That is the person who is ill, who accepts healing energy, perhaps on a subconscious level, and recovers. Or, we could say that, ultimately, the healer is God. The third party, that we may believe is the healer, is really a help, but not the actual healer."

This view is consistent with the beliefs of other healers, some of whom put much of their own energy into intense, intricate visualizations of bodily systems returning to normal equilibrium. However, the persons who recover from illness, their families and their friends may want to credit the healer or God. There are even other healers who say that they do not know how healing works. It is enough for them to know that it does work.

Cliff says that giving or receiving healing is only one example of our mental abilities.

"The potential of the human mind is unlimited. I believe that there was a time in human history when we could do many more things such as literally fly without undue conscious effort. We, as human beings, have lost much of our knowledge and many of our abilities.

"There are many unusual things in our world that can not be logically explained by our present knowledge. The Coral Castle in Florida is a modern example of a mystery that links us to our lost history."

Today the Coral Castle is a Florida landmark and tourist attraction. Its original name was Rock Gate Park. It is truly a wonder and a mystery of the modern world. Its existence was first known in the 1930s when its owner, who was a private person, decided to move it from Florida City, because a new subdivision was planned nearby. In 1936 he bought 10 acres of land 10 miles away in Homestead. He then spent the next three years moving the structures.

The website says that a visitor to the castle at one time would have been greeted enthusiastically by a man weighing a mere 100 pounds and standing just over five feet tall. He would have asked for 10 cents admission and explained his fantasy world carved out of stone.

This man was Edward Leedskalnin, who was born in Riga, Latvia in 1887. When he was 26 years old, he was engaged to be married but his fiancée cancelled the wedding just one day before the ceremony. Heartbroken, he began to create a monument to his lost love, without any outside assistance or large machinery. He carved and sculpted more than 1,100 tons of coral rock. Amazingly, he used only hand tools to cut and move huge blocks, of unspecified size, out of the shoreline.

The coral along the shoreline was reportedly 4,000 feet thick in places.

Since no one ever witnessed the labor, some say he had supernatural powers. He took great pride in his work. He would say only that he knew the secrets used to build the ancient pyramids and if he could learn them, you could too.

One anecdote about the moving process has him standing beside a truck, with a huge block on the ground. The driver left for a few minutes and returned to find the old man sitting on the edge of the truck and the block on the back.

*

If a modern person, mystery man or not, is solely responsible for this creation, what about the ancient pyramids which exist in several countries around the world?

"I believe that the pyramids were built by mind power. I do not believe that levitation was difficult for some beings. It requires a comprehensive understanding that everything on this planet is connected. Also that nothing is solid. Everything is fluid. When you have the proper realization of this, you can move things. If you know how to do it, then it is no big deal."

A recent incident with a poltergeist in a nearby city is another example of the power of the human mind.

Cliff defines poltergeist as a physical emanation of energy, whether spirit-oriented or from some living human being. The intensity of someone's thoughts, and how strongly a person holds onto those thoughts, can project energy into the environment. Some persons can switch suddenly from a pleasant mood to intense anger. This can create strong energy which can cause such things as pictures to fall off walls or objects to break.

"We surrounded the place with an imaginary light with the intention of the poltergeist activity moving on. It stopped for a while and then resumed."

It has been decided that the disturbances are coming from one resident at the location. Since it is not considered spiritual in origin, a priest said that he had done all that he could and he would not return.

"We have no sense of spirit there. We believe this person is causing these things because of certain personal problems."

*

What is the relationship between The Echo and Cliff and Linda?

Linda says that "We believe that The Echo are also there to help us. We are protected from a spiritual aspect. It started after we had been together only a few months. As I was leaving our apartment in Niagara Falls on one occasion, I felt love and sensed that everything will be just fine. I was going to drive out of the parking lot when a woman backed her car with such force into the driver's side of my car, that the collision pushed my car over to the right at least six to eight feet. I was inside my car, but the investigating police still could not understand how I was alive. I had a backache for about a week, but I was okay. The Echo were protecting me."

Linda has a 12-year-old nephew in Vancouver named Brandon. He seems to bring out the best in other persons. Even without meeting him, Linda and Cliff have felt love for him and love from him.

"We have felt love for him from day one," says Linda.

"Even though we have never met him.

"We asked The Echo why we feel so much love for him. The Echo said that we feel love because Brandon is part of The Echo. He reincarnated because he wanted to help my mother and sister by encouraging them to love. He is loving and kind and considerate. He loves them and they love him."

Doctors told his mother when Brandon was born that they foresaw such a difficult life for him that perhaps it would be better not to let him live. His mother refused to follow their advice. He was born with his heart on the wrong side of his body. He is missing several organs. His lungs are too small.

He is in constant pain every day. He uses a wheelchair after once using a walker, which operated by the weight of his body. Despite many operations and much time in hospital, where the nurses love him, he still has several health problems.

Brandon is approximately 30 inches tall and weighs only about 24 lbs. Yet he is a happy, outgoing person. He is enthusiastic about life and sharing love with those around him. He is called intelligent. He is called bright. However, understandably, he feels isolated at school.

The producers of an American television show heard about Brandon and invited him to appear a few times, as the son of one of the main characters. He enjoyed the experience of being on a television program. The poignancy of his presence exceeded the drama of any fictional device.

Linda and Cliff send him love and healing regularly. They have talked to him on the telephone. They have visualized and remotely viewed him. Two other persons, practicing remote viewing with Cliff and Linda, reported similar impressions, without knowing anything about him. One reported feeling physical difficulties but also a sense of love. Another reported looking forward from Brandon's perspective and visualizing arms resting on horizontal supports with straps or other fittings.

"We think that he has a great spiritual awareness. People are grateful that he has been able to bring love for this long. To bring love seems to be his whole reason for being here. Especially for my mother. She shows him love above everything else."

*

Does Cliff think there is a new era of increased spirituality?

"I think that it is a dream of spiritually oriented people that the whole world is eventually going to become spiritual. I think the reality is that people are starving as they were 50 years ago, and some people are killing others for no reason other than that they think it is right. I have not seen any great change. Right now in Canada and the United States, the average person seems more concerned with things than with other people. Especially in the last 15 years, there seems to be a constant drive for people to invest and accumulate more money or wealth. More material things. It creates a holding mentality rather than a sharing or giving mentality. Material things are neutral. It depends what people do with them and whether or not people become obsessed with things.

"Our collective minds are still living in the 16th century. The idea that our conscious thinking can save our world, I believe, is possible. I am not sure I believe it will be done. I think that if we continue the way the general population is acting, in 200 years this planet will not be habitable.

"We have a society based on greed and oil. Oil is rapidly coming to an end. It will peak in the year 2020. After that it will be downhill, depleting oil supplies. There are alternative technologies if we bother to develop them. The development is political. Reducing pollution may be expensive but what is the alternative? Not being able to live on the planet? It is a frightening thought.
"There is much greed. The people in power are going to do everything they can to hold on to power. If there is talk of spiritual things, they turn their backs and walk away.
"We could put a mental protection around the planet but it would probably not be effective."

*

Is there a spiritual push to raise human awareness?

"I think Spirit is out to make a positive change in mankind. It all boils down to the free choice of human beings, whether or not they accept positive energies such as love.

*

Is there a spiritual push for more communication between the spiritual realm and the physical realm? For example, through more channelers.

"When I started channeling, there were only two channelers in Ontario. Some others got in and out of it. There are many more now."

Chapter 3   It takes a psychic to know a psychic

The title of this chapter could refer to Cliff or Linda in either order. Each has experienced psychic phenomena and learned to accept these things as their individual lives progressed. Also as their life together progressed. Each feels completed by the other. Each has memories of other lives together in different roles. After they realized this, they asked The Echo for confirmation. The answer was more than 1,500 other lives together.

They say they know about only the lives that they remember. They are more interested in this life, so they have not asked for much more information.

Linda says that, in one of her memories, she and Cliff are woodsmen in Britain. At about age 20 Linda is caught by soldiers and bound, and then they put out his (Linda's) eyes. They are about to set him (Linda) on fire but Cliff mercifully shoots a fatal arrow into him (Linda).
 Linda says that she has had the impression that her spirit then went out of body and saw the other woodsman (Cliff). Her spirit thought that he was a friend. The Echo said that they were twin brothers.

Another impression seems to be from the late 1800s in North Dakota. Cliff is the father. Linda is his son, aged about 16. His (Linda's) mother told him to look for his father in a snow storm. She says that she remembers seeing his hands and arms, as the Cliff father lay under a fallen tree. The son did not know that his father's back was broken. He inadvertently killed the father while dragging him to a clearing he had made in the snow, which he thought would be safe for his father.

Cliff says that he has memories of another life in which he worked in dungeons in France.

"I laid on hot irons and I stretched people. Now we think this is bad, but it was accepted then. It was just a job."

Cliff and Linda have taught past-life workshops. He says the main purposes are to demonstrate that the soul is eternal and to provide insight into a person's identity in this life. Some may become fascinated with the idea of a certain past life, to the neglect of certain aspects of this life, or to overlooking the overall pattern of development of their own eternal spirits.

"Let us say that someone was a silversmith. People may get caught up with the idea of previous occupations. They do not understand at first that a certain occupation from a certain life was only a very short time. The rest of their lives, they were other things. A pattern of a recurring occupation or interest may be more important because it could explain an interest in this life such as painting. I think that this life is the one that people have to concentrate on because they are in it."

He says that past lives can affect a person in this life only if he "carries baggage" into this life from the other lives. A person would benefit by leaving any negativity or misunderstanding behind in the other life, at all levels of awareness, and start fresh in this life. Each life is separate. No one is expected to relive past difficulties.

"There is a danger that memories may be used by an individual in a manner that is not beneficial in this life."

This leads to the concept of Karma. Some think that it is a process of retribution for past misdeeds. Another view is that we will be presented with the same lessons over and over until we learn our lessons and grow spiritually. Each view suggests that it accumulates from each life.

Cliff thinks that Karma develops and remains within one existence. The Echo also present this view.

"If I do negative or positive it will catch up with me before I leave this life. Memory may bring such things as a personal outlook, attitudes, feelings, and beliefs from other lives, but this is not Karma."

*

How do Cliff and Linda complement each other?

"To start with, Cliff has always said that we are equal. This is a pleasant change from the way that I was raised and from my first marriage, which now seems like another lifetime," Linda says. "Cliff never criticizes me, or rarely."

Cliff says that they complement each other's interests and strengths. They have some shared psychic interests and some different psychic interests. In addition to channeling, he has given clairvoyant readings and tarot card readings. Linda has directed Cliff's channeling sessions for approximately 25 years, after directing another channeler before Cliff. She practices numerology and has also done Reiki and palmistry. Together, they send healing energy to persons who are ill or troubled.

Linda started experiencing psychic phenomena at an early age. This was the occasion on which she first transported her body. She would do it again years later. It was difficult learning to accept and understand such experiences. (See Book One.)

Another incident is the occasion in which her parents thought she knew more than she should about her sister's leaving home.

"I was telepathic with my sister. In effect, I could see through her eyes when she was angry with my mother. When I was 17, my sister had left home. I could see that she was okay and I told our parents. However, our parents were concerned. They decided that I had helped her run away and that I knew where she was.

"The next day I felt that my sister was absolutely terrified. I sensed where I could go to help her. There was a huge raven on the ground. I sent it away. Then I comforted my sister.

"Things started to happen for me. I could look at photographs of people and tell what they are like. I could pick up people's feelings when they came near me. I was not 100 per cent accurate so I had doubt about this ability.

"Cliff and I have a telepathic thing between us. It used to irritate me. After I figured out something, and told Cliff, he said he instantly understood it the way I did, after I had spent all the time deciding about it. He could sense the thought process that I had used.

"This is one of the things that we have experienced. When you love someone, the two of you are telepathic. If there is anger or any kind of upset, it puts a wall between you and hinders the telepathy," says Linda. "If Cliff was upset, he could not tune in to me, but I could always tune in to Cliff despite any negative feelings."

Linda was angry and frustrated, during her recovery from encephalitis, that she could not always remember words and express herself. She realized that she had to visualize what she wanted to say. Cliff had to learn to open sufficiently to receive her ideas and understand what she wanted to say to him, despite his upset feelings at the time.

Linda has since thought a lot about her experience with encephalitis in 1994, during part of which she might have been considered clinically dead. She has had a range of thoughts and emotions. She is even able to be whimsical, counting the years since 1994 to say how old she is now.

One psychic event in which they worked together, or worked with a benign force, such as a spirit guide, took place in the early 1980s, at a psychic fair in a mall in east Toronto.

"It was a poor location for a psychic fair because it was in gang territory. We also had a tape recorder stolen in that nasty spot, so we left on the second day of the scheduled five days," says Cliff.

"I had stepped away from our booth and I was returning as Linda was doing a reading. I saw some teenagers on the second floor mezzanine. One leaned out with a soft drink, trying to align it over Linda's head. Then he dropped it.

"I yelped when I saw the container falling down, but it curved in the air, moved off and hit the floor, about two feet away from Linda.

"The drink did not hit Linda at all. It poured around her and she did not realize that it could have hit her."

On the occasion of another psychic experience, Linda was fully aware of what Cliff was seeing, because she could see the same thing.

In September, 1998, Cliff's mother passed away at the age of 89. The funeral took place in her hometown of Aurora, north of Toronto. After Cliff and Linda arrived at the funeral home, they saw the spirit of Cliff's deceased mother standing in a corner of the room containing her coffin.

Linda says that the apparition looked much younger, about 35 years of age. Cliff concurs that the apparition looked much younger.

They did not elbow each other at the time for confirmation of the strange sight and they did not say anything to Cliff's sister.

"Mentioning what we saw would have freaked my sister right out, but Linda and I talked about it after," says Cliff.

"We realized that the apparition wore the same kind of clothing as we described to each other. We knew that we had seen the same image.

"It gave me verification," Linda says with a laugh.

"That was important to me."

Another incident, in Hamilton, a city west of Toronto, might have brought smiles to the faces of the especially sensitive among those who were paying their respect at the funeral home.

"As I recall, it was before a wake, at least 20 years ago. The somber attendant asked who we were there to see. His attitude became almost dismissive when we told him. With a gesture toward a certain room, he told us where we could find the people that we wanted to visit.

"There was laughing and joking at the door of the room. We heard upbeat music playing when we opened the door. It was like walking into a festival. Everyone was laughing, carrying on, and celebrating the life of our friend's mother. She had been in a lot of pain and discomfort so they were happy that she was now at peace. A minister was officiating."

The final detail is that a recognizable apparition of the mother of the friend was sitting on the coffin, swinging her legs, and making faces at the minister, during the funeral service. The empty shell of her body lay inside the coffin.

"She didn't really have any truck with ministers," says Cliff with a smile.

Cliff thinks that most people could "see things" because it is only a matter of being tuned into whatever frequency is necessary.

Linda says that the first time she saw somebody who had just crossed over was her ex-husband's grandmother.

It was in Newmarket, a town at the time, now a city, north of Toronto.

"Bob and I were going to a funeral. The room was gloomy. Everything was grey. I saw Bob's grandfather sitting in front of the coffin. There were people sitting beside him. He was crying. I saw a woman standing next to him and she had her hand on his shoulder. When she turned and looked at me, I could see through her. She started to walk toward me. I knew it was Bob's grandmother who had crossed over because she saw that I saw her. He then started to cry really loudly because she no longer had her hand on his shoulder.

"She stopped walking toward me, turned, went back and put her hand on his shoulder again. With this, his crying became softer again."

Another incident involved a requested sign rather than a sighting. After Linda's brother was killed in an automobile accident, Linda, who was 26 at the time, and her Aunt Pauly went to the funeral home.

"There were drapes in the room and a sheet over the coffin. So I said, 'John, if there is life after death, show me by making the curtains move.'

"Suddenly the curtains moved. Aunt Pauly and I left the room very quickly," says Linda.

A third incident involved an unrequested sign.

Linda was staying at her parents' home for her cousin's wedding near Trenton, a town east of Toronto.

"My friend Gail and I were talking until 2-3 a.m. in one of the two upstairs bedrooms. The air force homes were two-storey saltboxes, with stairs leading up the centre between the two rooms.

"We suddenly heard somebody coming upstairs. I opened the door to see who it was, but no one was there. My mother said later that it was just my deceased brother John wanting to see who was there."

Linda says that she has had a lot of experiences with her younger brother John, since his sudden passing in the automobile accident.

"I once had a curling sweater that John liked so much that I let him borrow it. When he returned it, he had messed it up so much that I said he could keep it.

"About 1969-70 I had a dream in which John was wearing that curling sweater. He said that he was in school now and learning a lot. He said that everything is fine. Then in 1984, my mother and my sister, Carole, said that they each had had the same dream in which John was wearing that sweater. They had the dream around the same time as I did."

On one occasion when Cliff worked at Bernel in Buffalo, the four supervisors, including Cliff, were closing their area of the factory at midnight.

"The other three supervisors and I saw an unknown man walking down a main aisle between the blocks of foam. We saw him walk into the men's washroom. We heard the door open and slam. Three of us converged on the washroom because we wanted to know who he was.

"When we looked inside there was no one in the washroom. The windows were locked. We never found out who it was. All four of us saw this mysterious apparition from different perspectives, from the different areas of the plant that we had been in," says Cliff.

"There have been many instances in our lives in which we have had such sudden contact with Spirit.

"To the people who want to be debunkers, I say more power to them. However, they will never convince a person who has actually seen something that they were hallucinating or anything else. The reason is that those instances are extremely clear and remain in your mind forever. It is nothing like seeing your friend George on the street and 20 years later not being able to remember when you last saw George.

"When you encounter Spirit, it remains vivid in your mind for the rest of your life."

On one occasion Cliff, as a teenager, was walking home from a road south of Aurora.

"It was 11 pm and very dark. I was halfway through a cemetery, intending to pick up the train tracks on the other side and follow them home.

"Car headlights from neighboring Yonge Street would flash by every ten minutes or so. Not like every 10 seconds or so now. So when a car's lights illuminated the cemetery, I saw a man walking toward me about 10 feet away.

"He made a sound of surprise such as 'Eep' and I made the same sound of surprise such as 'Eep.'

"We passed each other. I took five or six steps and then I turned to look back at him but nobody was there at all.

"I was not frightened of that kind of thing, I was always interested. I would think: 'How did he do that?' "

Cliff says that people have mentioned to him that there were occasions on which they thought they had seen something inexplicable and they would be frightened.

"I was used to seeing things so I would think that just seeing something has no effect on you. Why would you be afraid of something that you saw? If it walks over and hits you with a stick, that is a whole different story," he says.

Another example of overlapping perception occurred when Cliff and Linda lived in Niagara Falls. One day, Linda was meditating while Cliff was out.

"I had a tendency to look through Cliff's eyes when I was meditating to know where he was and how he was. Once I saw his hand reaching down to a doorknob in the hallway of our apartment building. I did not think anything of it because it was a natural image when I was meditating.

"Then when the door opened and Cliff came into the room, it surprised the living daylights out of me. I thought it was my imagination. I did not expect him actually to walk through the doorway.

"Anyway, after that if I wanted to know where he was, I knew that all I had to do was enter an altered state. It helped because I did not worry about him when he was out."

Psychics can also work together in practical ways. On one December morning, probably in 1982, Cliff and Linda were sleeping late after being out the previous evening. Linda liked having the windows open overnight for fresh air.

Cliff got out of bed about 9 a.m. to answer the telephone. It was the local radio station asking whether he could be a last-minute substitute guest for a call-in program. As he was listening to the caller and agreeing to help as a guest, he realized that the townhouse felt cold compared to his warm bed. He was not wearing any clothing and could see that the bedroom windows were open.

"Shortly, I started doing clairvoyant readings over the air for the program's callers. As Linda realized that I was not going to get back in bed, she started bringing me clothing items. Some one at a time.

"I was trying to get dressed, receive impressions and not disrupt things. I had to hold the phone carefully, concentrate on the program, and do the readings without shivering or losing my train of thought as I dressed."

Linda brought all of Cliff's clothing before she got dressed herself and made coffee. He has never told the host of the show about the incident. The callers had no inkling of the especially sensitive condition of their psychic reader that morning. Of all the radio programs that Cliff and Linda have done, they say that this was the most unusal experience for either one of them.

*

While Cliff can be described as straightforward and no-nonsense, Linda is readily accepting and forgiving.

"Linda is the only person in my entire life, that I see regularly, who never has anything bad to say about anyone. She sees the good in everyone," says Cliff.

"Before Cliff and I got together, I would see the negative things in people first, then maybe I would see the positive. With Cliff doing the channeling, I have the love of The Echo all around me. It is the type of questions asked and the information given. The Echo see things in a different way and as a result, it helped me, most of the time, to stop judgmentalism," says Linda.

"I can love the spirit or God part of other persons, even if I am not able to like them. It helps remove judgmentalism. I can send them love and peace. I can pray for them. However, we do not have to be around difficult persons or associate with them. We can put an invisible field around ourselves to keep negative people and bad influences away from us."

*

Linda maintains her positive attitude even in traffic.

"I know how other drivers are feeling and how they are going to move their car. How fast they will go or when they will slow down. One reason I do not get angry is that I know how they are feeling. I know they want freedom if they have been feeling trapped. My being empathetic has helped us avoid accidents."

Cliff says, "Another driver can cut us off four times in a row. Linda will say maybe he's late for work. I will trust Linda's feelings implicitly on the highway. She may say maybe we should get off the highway. Take an alternate route. We do. We may find out later there has been an accident or traffic was just jammed."

However, Cliff admits to having less patience than Linda.

"I have turned off some people in the past because I would be upset at other drivers on the road. I am as human as the next person. I live in a physical world and, therefore, have to be physical. As the driver of our vehicle, I was simply venting frustration. I have not wished anyone harm and I never would.

"However, some people may find my behavior offensive because I am in a spiritual field of work. Anytime a spiritual leader or teacher openly acts in the opposite manner, it may turn off some of the persons they know. I can keep the physical and spiritual sides of life separate. I believe that there would have to be a lot of deliberate negativity to hamper being open to the spiritual," he says.

Despite her strong belief in The Echo, at one time Linda was reluctant to ask personal questions about her marriage with Cliff.

"Cliff and I were married about two years. I became hypoglycemic. We had a life on the psychic fair circuit. Meals at midnight. Coffee. This went on for five or six months.

After a long weekend in September, I thought that if I just remove sugar from my diet I will be okay. But my personality changed. I became difficult over the slightest thing.

"I did not ask The Echo about my health or this change because I always thought that psychics gave information through their own feelings. I was worried that Cliff might have thought he had married the wrong person again.

"I had become very difficult. I still felt hypoglycemic even though I had taken sugar out of my diet. I felt that my future was black.

"On one occasion another couple had finished asking their questions at an Echo session. I was directing, so I asked how much more time we had. The Echo said that Cliff could stay in trance for another 10-15 minutes. I thought Cliff was so deep in trance on that occasion that I would get a good answer, if I simply asked.

"I felt reassured and confident that I could finally ask my question. I said that I had a personal question. The Echo replied, 'We thought you would never ask.'

"So when I started to ask, they said that I was hypoglycemic. They recommended that I become a complete vegetarian. They said that the future would look gray for three days, rather than black. Then after three months the future would look bright. It happened as they said it would. After that occasion, I felt freer to ask more questions about myself."

Another of Linda's psychic talents is to communicate with animals telepathically. This ability to use telepathy to communicate with animals is becoming more accepted today.

Cliff learned a method of connecting minds with dogs from Linda.

"If there was a dog that was barking or snarling at us, Linda would send her thoughts to it and the dog would settle down. One Sunday afternoon we stopped to look in the window of a motorcycle shop. There was a Doberman guard dog sitting on the porch of the neighboring house. The dog was just going nuts. Barking and snarling and showing its teeth.

"Linda looked at the dog and sent her feelings. The dog quieted, turned its back on us and sat down. Occasionally, it looked over its shoulder and said 'woof.'

Linda says what she "was getting from the dog was that he had not to see us to stop barking. So this is what he did.

"Part of me touches the minds of animals and I receive impressions. I always send love and they let me send it to them. They open up to me.

"People are telepathic with animals. In telepathic communication, we can train animals and give them ideas. However, bad dogs reject it. I send love but it does no good."

On one occasion in Vancouver, Cliff thought that if a mad dog advances another step, he would kill it. The dog sensed Cliff's determination and it backed down.

Once in St. Catharines, as a parking bylaw enforcement officer, Cliff sent a message to a dog that it would not be a good idea to attack him. It quieted as its owner worked himself up, although the owner was in the wrong. The owner became more upset than the dog.

"Why did some persons become upset when I had to ticket their vehicles for illegal parking?

"People see it as negative social judgment and being caught is difficult for them to accept.

"When we lived in the Northwest Territories, I was driving around Rankin Inlet with an Inuit man who was also a dog owner. We saw one of my dogs running loose on the street. So I stopped the truck and whistled for my dog. The Inuit man said that my dog will never return. After a husky gets loose, it is gone.

"I whistled twice and not only did my dog return, it jumped into our vehicle and sat between us.

"I was thinking that this dog is my friend. I was sending feelings of love to it."

It was in the in the Northwest Territories (now Nunuvut) that Linda learned that she can communicate telepathically with dogs.

They taught their dogs to pull a sled with Linda leading the way on the snowmobile and sending a mental picture of what she wanted of the dogs. Cliff drove the sled.

On a day that they were using a one-two-two-two formation, one of the dogs in the second two was not pulling its weight. The lead dog stopped the team. It turned back, jumped over the first pair of dogs and trounced the slacker. Cliff thought it was a fight and he wanted to stop it. Linda said the lead dog was just using a form of discipline. Soon order returned as the chastened dog co-operated.

Linda's influence with dogs was also useful when she taught a mother dog how to take an occasional break from her nursing puppies. Linda visualized on only one occasion, the dog jumping on top of the dog house and then jumping on top of the wire fence and walking over the top of the next section of the pen and then jumping down to the ground. She visualized the dog returning by the opposite route. The dog quickly learned what Linda pictured.

*

Does being close to animals come from their psychic background?

"We see animals as thinking, functioning beings. Once, after a pet dog had died, it came to me in my dreams.

"Animals are part of God. Every animal is different. Some dogs are even drawn to you from previous lives," says Linda.

***

Cliff has been interested in painting, drawing and sketching since childhood. He has completed dozens of paintings and framed a couple dozen of the most appropriate. His oil paintings, of landscapes and nature scenes of different parts of Canada, hang on walls, appropriately, in different parts of Canada. There is a painting on his dining room wall of the Bow River in Alberta. He painted it from a photograph in the early 1960s. He painted a gliding hawk in Rankin Inlet, Nunuvut, from memory. This painting hangs on his living room wall. Among the paintings he has sold is a nature scene of two wolves on a shoreline in Fort Frances, in northern Ontario. Many others have been given as gifts.

"Painting is a form of self-expression and gives me a sense of saving something on canvas that may not exist in another 50 years. I have as much satisfaction from painting as from my other interests but it is a different kind of satisfaction. I imagine it is a similar satisfaction to what a potter has when he creates something.

"I used to lock myself in the attic in Fort Erie (Ontario) for two days because I had become involved in my painting.

"When I have an urge to paint, I have a tingling sensation in my fingers and I have to pick up a brush. I have not studied any styles. I attempt to put on canvas what I see, whether in my mind or in front of me.

He says he is self-taught except for one day. On that day, he went to a recognized artist in Fort Erie, and he asked her for lessons. She instructed him to go out into the countryside and paint a barn. So Cliff set up his canvas in front of a barn and he filled the canvas with an oil painting of a barn. When the instructor saw it, she said that she had not meant that he paint just the barn. Her disapproval of his personal effort ended his formal training.

***

Cliff's life-long interest in motorcycles led to his acquiring a license in 1981. Then he put a magazine picture of a motorcycle on the wall of his home in Niagara Falls. He visualized the bike as his. He kept the photograph for a couple of years. One day his son phoned him, although he had not seen the picture, and asked whether Cliff wanted the smaller of the son's two motorcycles. Thus he bought his first motorcycle from his son.

"I had wanted one for a long time. I get a sense of freedom from motorcycling. I liken it to riding horses across the prairies. Just being out in nature, experiencing the wind, sun and rain. You can be nimble on the road even at high speeds."

They had an ATV, a three-wheeler, in Rankin Inlet as their family vehicle in the summer. They drove a snowmobile in the winter. Cliff sold a motorcycle he owned in Fort Frances before they moved south. He complained for a couple of years that he had no motorcycle so Linda's son finally gave him a cabinet-top model of a motorcycle. He was told that he had to stop griping. Then Cliff bought his current motorcycle.

"After we moved back to Niagara, we searched for people to ride with. We tried one area motorcycle club but they mostly wanted to drink beer and be rowdy. A year later we heard about another club. After a year of attending meetings at that club, we became chapter directors for two years."

**** Part 2 ****

The Echo

Original transcripts of channeling sessions

As I was writing this book in September, 2005, I told The Echo during one channeling session the type of information that I planned to use, including their regular message that " Love is the only answer." I asked what other information they would like to be in this book.

The Echo replied:

The understandings of the individual empowerment of each and every entity…of the esteem factors that the society in which thee exist tend to denigrate.

There be the presenting of the understandings of the oneness of the universe, of the individualism of each entity, yet maintaining the connection of the oneness of the universe.

That the human animal is neither created nor destroyed, that it merely change form of occasion as it move forward to the totality of understanding and return to Godhead.

This be major understanding that be necessary for the human animal to progress - that the removal of judgmentalism be imperative.

That the consideration for all others in the physical realm be imperative.

That consideration for the, here refer, the atmosphere of the environment of thee which thee create be imperative.

These understandings be all part and parcel in which we have approached in order to teach the physical entities of the planet.

Love reigns supreme. That hate…angers…be self-depreciating and withhold entity from its positive growth patterns, oftimes causing an entity to repeat a particular existence format. Oftimes repeating an entire incarnation in order to learn the lessons of love.

Chapter 4
The Echo, God, humanity's past and future

October 12, 2005
St. Catharines, Ontario

Present: Cliff Preston, channeling The Echo
Linda Preston, directing the session
Author, asking questions for this book.

Author:
The first question that I would like to ask Golude, the speaker, and The Echo, the group, is, "Who are you?"

The Echo:
That of the term, refer, Golude be merely an identification for the understanding of those within the physical realm. That of the energy of, that refer, Golude have existed in, that here refer, prior times. The entity have existed approximate, in thy terms of time understanding, years 35,000 prior of present. Here the entity be in the involvement, in thy terms, of the psychology of the human animal and the assistance to human animals through the use of, that refer, psychologies, understandings, the color therapies, and discussions of human animals.

That of the form, that be referred to, the Golude, have chosen to remain incarnate, as it find the opportunity to further assist through this format of, here refer, channeling, you understand. There be in contact availability to that of the spirit energy, refer, Golude, that of an near-uncountable resource of spirit entity energies. The entity Golude in the attempt to find informations for an questioner in the physical realm then send request out to the atmosphere, to the spirit realm, to ask those that be in, here refer, light energy format, to offer solutions or answers from their perspectives. In this manner, that of the energy force Golude, is able to send some informations through that of the physical body of the form Clifford and forward these informations to those in the physical format that be in question, you understand.

Linda:
Could you talk a little on color therapy?

The Echo:
It be associated most to that of the presentation of colored light directed to an individual, singular light, such as, here refer, purple for the ague symptoms. Blue for that of lethargy. Yellows for that of depression format. There also be used that of the mineral baths that be lighted from beneath and indeed be dyed to, that refer, the color necessary for the individual.

Author:
Golude seems to be alone in the foreground. Everyone else in the group seems to be in the background. I thought that the whole group called The Echo was in the foreground. Has anything changed?

The Echo:
Indeed not. The whole group be a huge conglomerate of light energy spirits that may offer informations that be requested through the form of the one Golude.

Author:
I believe when Cliff started channeling, there were approximately 5,000 spirits. It increased, perhaps to 50,000, and has increased to now "uncountable"?

The Echo:
Near-uncountable.

Answer:
Would it be for example 100,000 plus?

The Echo:
We would prefer, hmn, 100 million plus.

Author:
That is progress. (Laughing)

Now I would like to ask a number of questions about God. That is our term. The one word expresses a lot of ideas. It expresses the source. Or it expresses love…you know who I am referring to when we say God.

The Echo:
Hmn. Indeed. We say God who? You understand. Each individual entity, be it physical or spiritual, is God within its own being. Firstly here understand that which thee refer God. God is an term that have been applied, by that of the creatures, refer, men to explain that which they have no means of explaining. It be an term that be presented to, refer, to that which is unexplainable. Example, that point in time as you know here, here … hmn, hmn, ah…state Year One, in thy present calendar understanding. Here the entities may encounter that of a severe weather pattern. Example thunderstorms, dust storms in the desert, and the entities do not understand how these storms occur, where the storms come from, why the storms beset them so dramatically. The entities then state that this must needs be caused by that of a great spirit which is displeased or discontent or wishing to present an idea to they. This then have grown through generations of humans in order to explain all manner of phenomena in occurrence about them. Therefore understand God is merely an term. However, within thy learned understanding, that which thee refer God is the energy force of the universe and is inherent in all creatures and in all humans that exist within the universe.

Author:

OK. There is another word I was just writing down. By God, I mean the creator, the source, the universal mind. You called it the energy force of the universe. Does God change or grow?

The Echo:
Indeed not. Even in that of the weak efforts of the human entities, they have come to explain that matter can not be created nor destroyed. Since that of the ... here, oh ... definition of God be the energy of the universe, it remain constant at all times.

Linda:
Some people feel that Jesus is speaking through them. Some people believe them and others think it is ridiculous. When people say Jesus or God is speaking through them, what do you say about that?

The Echo.
Yes, indeed.

Linda:
"Yes, indeed"? You have given the information on how everyone is God, but how can this be said in a way that other people accept?

The Echo:
You understand that of the human mind may be here likened to that which refer radio, you understand. Do radio be tuned to an particular frequency it then is in contact with a particular discussion or particular musics. The human mind is somewhat similar. Do the human mind be tuned, as it were, to an particular frequency, it then receive informations from that frequency. In that of thy query, thee state that there be those that feel that Jesus be speaking through them. Indeed so, be of fine format. For these entities have attuned their minds to receive the informations from that entity.
However, they may also attune their minds to receive the energies from ... oh, in thy colloquial terms, Tom, Dick or

Harry, you understand. It be merely that the entities have learned through their social environs that the form refer Jesus, Hesu, speak with great importance. Therefore, it be of greater ... oh, response, as imagined, to speak to that refer Hesu. However, that refer Tom, Dick, or Harry may also give thee similar informations and indeed of similar value.

Linda:
Would you then also comment on people that have been called saints?

The Echo:
Indeed so. Thee may call anyone saint.

Linda:
The Church decides.

The Echo:
Indeed so. Thee have answered thy own query. The church decides.

Linda:
But what these saints have had occur, were they actually channeling?

The Echo:
Indeed, you understand. These entities, prior stated, have indeed tuned their minds to particular frequencies of information and in passing the information to the human race, may ... oh, find rejection or castigation oftimes due to the simple fact that those listening enter into, here refer, jealous format for they find themselves unable to perform similar. Therefore it must needs in order to maintain that of controls, or that of status, it then behoove entities to denigrate another, and that is somewhat easier matter if the other is speaking of previously unknown events or facts.

Author:
Some religions suggest that human beings can disappoint or anger God. So my question is...Can human beings hurt God, lessen God, help God or increase God?

Echo
Hmn. No...No...No.

(Laughter)

Author:
OK. Then why is it suggested that a person should be loving and considerate and help others? If this is not to help God, it is to help the individual?

The Echo:
Indeed. You understand. This have not have to do with, that refer, God, in reality. This then social concept of behavior in relation to others in thy social format. You understand an entity in one land may ...oh, arbitrarily kill another entity if it be thought the other entity have overstepped an social bound. In another land it is forbidden to kill anyone. And understand forbidden is a social concept word.
Therefore, be in awareness that of the social atmosphere in which an entity exist will dictate its entity belief system. Any belief system is derived from watching, learning, growing within an social environment. Do an entity be, here refer, in growth alone in a forest for its lifetime and have not contact of other humans in any form, the entity will have no understanding of good, bad, evil, loving or any other aspect that is socially related. The entity will merely exist, feed its being, take care of its own being and will never experience such things as guilt or despise of other creatures.
Author:
Could you tell us then the purpose of humanity?

The Echo:
Indeed. The purpose of humanity is to eat, grow, to procreate, in order for the species to continue. The purpose of humanity is no

different from that of the purpose of a lion, or the purpose of an hedgehog. It is merely life in the living. And that of the, here refer, other aspects that which be termed greatness, that which be termed high achievement, the building of bridges, the building of tall structures, the creation of roads, definitions of science. All these aspects, be separate and apart from the reality of the physical existence of humans. It be, refer in thy colloquial terms ... oh 'window dressing'. When an entity, for example, places upon that of ... oh, thy term, Christmas tree, the Christmas tree be festooned, decorated and be made beautiful for the celebration of social significance, yet it remain a tree.

Linda:
A number of years ago you said living in our physical world is like a school. When you say it is like a school for us, could you talk about that?

The Echo:
That of the, here refer, recurring existences of the human entity. Be indeed much as, that refer, school. The entity be, here refer, striving to attain fulfillment, knowledge, understanding, and indeed that of the development of love. Firstly, the love of self. This then through the learnings, the growings in repeated incarnational format bring the entities to the point of understanding in which they no longer have a need within to reincarnate. The entity then become one with, that refer, the universal energies about thee. This be that which man have referred to as that of the Godhead.

Author:
Echo, I am going to back up. I am going to ask you this question: What was the purpose of the creation of humanity? Why did human beings start? Why did they come about?

The Echo:

Indeed that of the, refer, creation be lost in that of the mists of time. For that of the human animal have existed physically upon that of the planet, refer Earth, for that of hundreds of millions of years. There have been growths and declines. There have been societies in growths and declines, as is the present society in decline. However the settlement, primary settlement of that of the planet Earth, be an transposition of entities that be deemed unsuitable or somewhat ill from that, here refer, other areas of the universe. These entities have a lack of, that refer, green resonance in their auras and this cause they to be violent in nature. Have angry format, and these entities, be as it were, sent to the planet Earth as, in thy terms as a ... oh holding center, as a prison, as it were. The entities then be left to ... oh develop the selves to learn, to grow, and to gradually reinstate that of the, here refer, green lacking within the aura. This be of an approximate 35 to 45,000 of years prior of present. There do be individuals existing on the planet Earth prior to this implantation format. However it be of large implantation occurrences approximately 35-45,000 of years prior of present.

Author:
Echo, I have read that God is a static perfection and human beings were created to experience for God and send back the nature of the experiences to God, because God can not experience directly. Is that correct?

The Echo:
Indeed not within our terms of understanding. Those, refer, human beings, experience for human beings. And for that connection to spirit which may be termed oversoul, for each entity. Understand this be an individual learning path format.

Author:
I am coming at you from a different angle because I can't quite get the type of information that I want.

The Echo:
Indeed so.

Author:
OK. This is a give-and-take session. I am just trying to say that if God is perfect and complete, if God lacks for nothing and needs nothing...why then were human beings created? Was there a lack in God? Was there a lack in the universe? Why would there be human beings? If God was already there, why create human beings?

The Echo:
Indeed. Have already stated to thee that God is that energy force which is inherent in each and every entity. It be not, here refer, separate and apart. That, oh ... in reply to thy query: Why were human beings created? Because the energy forces have chosen conscious emanation and this be presented in the form of the human animal.

Linda:
Echo, once you described this as an ocean and each of us a drop in the ocean. So if somebody changes, it affects everybody else.

The Echo:
To an degree, indeed so. You understand in reality there be none within the physical realm that be alone. They be physically separated perhaps, however, they be connected at all times through that of the mind, that of the ... oh, which thee refer the spirit realm, the Akashic record, the energies of they and these be all emanations of each separate entity drawn to the atmosphere and be in availability of ... oh, receptivity, of contact by any, you understand.

Author:
What I am hearing, Echo, is that the idea of a personal God is a human creation. Humanity is part of the energy of the universe. No one watches over us. Human beings create their own reality and existence, and are endeavoring to return to the Godhead, which is the universal energy, because, at some point,

consciousness decided to separate itself, to some degree, from that universal energy.

The Echo:
Indeed so. Understand as the entities be in the form of human, that of the decision to perform, grow, to develop in any pattern is an completely individual decision, you understand. For there be not here right or wrong. There be only growth, development and learning. The direction of learning and the direction of growth be not relevant to any entity except the one in process.

Author:
It almost seems like an experiment or adventure, when human beings came into existence. It happened because it could happen. From you, I am not getting a pre-ordained reason or an ultimate good that would be served by the creation of humanity, just that energy could become human beings, so it did.

The Echo:
Indeed so. You understand here, mushrooms grow because the conditions are correct for it. Humans began development because the conditions were correct for it.

Author:
I have read that human beings are parts of God, the universal energy. Say fragments of energy became a little adventurous and they wandered away from their original mentality and, in a sense, they lost their way because then they could not see the connection with the overall energy. Does that roughly describe humanity?

The Echo:
Indeed. Very few of those within the physical existence have an understanding of their connection to the rest of humanity.

Author:

I have two questions. How are human beings connected to God? I have another question what is the difference between human essence and divine essence. I think you are saying we are emanations or manifestations of divine essence or universal energy.

The Echo.
Indeed. Human essence, you understand, it be all one and the same. It be merely an manner of which it be viewed as correct use or incorrect use and, in our perception, is only use. You understand.

Author:
It is difficult for the human mind to understand… if we are part of God, the universal energy, did we exist after the energy, or always exist with the energy, always in a possible form, and at some point the possibility became reality, took on an independent consciousness?

The Echo.
Indeed. Highest degree of probability. That of the, here refer, origins be lost in, that refer, the mists of thy understandings in time.

Author.
From your point of view, farther up the hill, as you have described it, you do not see through the mist to the very beginning?

Echo.
Indeed not. This be also beyond we.

Author:
Is there any truth in the Adam and Eve story of creation? Is it a rough approximation of what happened to humanity at some point?

The Echo:

Indeed not. That of the Adam and Eve fable is indeed that - fable. This be brought to the attention of the peoples in order that the peoples gain an sense of, here refer, of propriety, and an sense of that which is to be considered right and wrong, and to be uh...in order that the social atmosphere be relatively peaceful and safe in which to exist That of the, here refer, Adam and Eve be an fable that be designed by an single developing culture and the other developing cultures that be upon the planet, at once and the same time, be then totally discounted for they be unknown to the perpetrators of the fable.

Linda:
When I was 12 I used to think that Adam and Eve...Eden was somewhere else. That is what they were talking about. That story of Eden was actually another planet. They were not very happy with me at church from that. When I wrote that little article "What If" you said that, approximately four and a half million years ago, we came to this planet as a prison. This seemed to me what the story of Adam and Eve was. They came to this planet as a prison and had to develop and grow from that.

The Echo.
Indeed. This be of fine understanding. That refer Adam and Eve story, as it be presented, is an, here, fable format. The fable may be derived from that of the ... hmn ... unconscious memory format of those creating the fable.

Author:
Echo, I think then that you are saying, of the three theories that are taught in schools about the origin of the human race... one is creationism, that is Adam and Eve, so you are saying forget that. The other two are evolution ... the idea that human beings have evolved from lower life forms, possibly even from single-celled creatures. And ... I am hearing more about intelligent design. I don't know whether it strictly addresses the beginning of humanity, but I think intelligent design says that there is a universal mind, or some reason, some purpose behind our life and it is not just meaningless chaos. Could you comment on the evolution theory and the intelligent design theory?

The Echo:
That of the, understand ... all these formats be indeed theory. Theory is an idea that is not yet proven, you understand. And uh, these theories of the development of the human animal from an amoeba at the bottom of the sea and gradual growth development to an land-walking animal is ... oh, oh ... difficult for we to understand...hmn ...the reasons behind such thinking.

Author:
I think then you are saying ... and Linda's question ...you are saying that planet Earth was colonized by human beings who have come from other planets.

The Echo:
Indeed so.

Author:
So, it is interesting that of all these theories taught in school, they do not teach colonization. Linda was trying to get that in there.

The Echo:
You understand, to teach colonization is to destroy religion. To destroy religion is to lose control of the masses.

Author:
But that also leaves us with a question. If we want to know the origin of the human race, and we, maybe, have a misconception that the human race originated on Earth and we have these two or three different theories. If someone else comes along and says it didn't originate on Earth, on another planet, colonized on Earth . So then we say: OK, so that's how we started on Earth but then we have the question: How did the human race originate on another planet? You are saying the answer is lost in the mists of time. So we will not pursue that one.

The Echo:

Indeed, you understand. Be not of concern. For, you understand, those within the physical reality of the present require only to understand their physical requirements of the present.

Author:
It could be suggested that we can think too much…or speculate too much… with no purpose or productivity in our thinking.

The Echo:
Indeed so. You understand, within that of the existence in the physical realm, there do be requirements. Due to the hairlessness of the physical human entity, it require warmth. It require sustenance. It require shelter. And …oh, oh …require in the present, it require social joining. Therefore, these be the major requirements of existence and to dwell upon that of the past is to stand still within thy developmental paths. To engage in the killing of each other is to stand still within thy developmental paths. Although the entities understand this be neither right nor wrong … for there be not of judgment of any entity, except in that of an social environment, you understand.

Author:
Then just one more question on the past. Since you mentioned that many civilizations have risen and fallen. Could you give us a little information about some civilizations that have risen and fallen? Perhaps Atlantis or Lemuria?

The Echo:
Indeed. Atlantis be society throughout the entire planet. Within thy present understanding concepts that of Atlantis must have been an island on the planet. You understand this be untrue. This be an society throughout the planet. This be, oh, as it were, self-destructed as these entities entered into experimentation with the creatures of the planet and in the delving into the energies of that, uh refer, the crystal energies and cause the Earth to shudder. And in the shuddering there be floodings, there be landslides, there be devastations of populations and indeed the devastation of the entire society, leaving individuals isolated and fending for selves and gradually

rebuilding an society requiring, in thy terms of understanding, hundreds of years to bring to fruitions, you understand.

Author:
You have said our present society is in decline. What are the most probable things that will happen to the human race between now and the year 2025? That is 20 years. My references are to social organization; government; the manufacturing and distribution of goods; the production and distribution of food; the weather; and in human thinking.

First, what are the most probable differences in social organization?

The Echo:
Indeed. The highest probability of changes in, that refer, social organization, be that the lands be under controls or near controls in an dictatorial format. That the major countries become more highly militaristic, and more highly controlling of their populations. That of individual freedoms be gradually disintegrated to that point of which to disagree is an violation. This be not in total effect, to that refer, 20 years. However, be well toward this format and this be universal in nature. Of the universal of the planet, in nature. That the populations be greatly controlled by those who state to know that which is best for all. And this then result in dictatorial format around the entire globe.

Author:
Why is this developing and is there a way to slow it or stop it?

The Echo:
Be developing due to decisions of those entities that be in power, or close to power positions, merely because they can. There be that of, refer, advertising campaigns to bring the public to accept less within their existences. Indeed this be in process of present as the entities that have created that of an understanding that smaller transportation devices indeed be of, referred, comparatively better for the public to use. This is an

general gradual means of creating thought patterns of acceptance of lesser within the lives of individuals. As is, that refer, housing format, such as in, that refer, North America to allow the building, here refer, long cohabitational buildings and this also create within the minds of individuals the acceptance of less within their existences. The freedom of choice related to such as the choosing of work positions or the choosing of living locations be gradually removed from individual choice patterns and this is in process at present.

Author:
OK. Then I have the manufacture and distribution of goods and the production and distribution of food. Will this be done in any great difference from today?

The Echo:
Within that of the 20-year span be not a great difference, but in thy comparative terms, greater governmental control.

Author:
Do you see more genetic modification of food or more organic and healthier food?

The Echo:
Indeed. There be an bent toward that refer, healthier foods. However, the healthier foods be controlled by the, presently refer, the drug organizations, and these organizations will indeed ... oh ... alter the, that refer, healthier foods, you understand.

Linda:
What about the vitamins and things like that. Is there still going to be accessibility to people?

The Echo:
To an, comparative, lesser degree.

Author:

I have heard that some companies that control the production and distribution of food are linked to the drug companies. They may want to keep customers for life by treating symptoms.

The Echo:
Indeed. Be of that, here refer, greed format. Indeed so.

Author:
I have a category about human thinking (laughing) but I don't think we want to say very much about that because I keep hearing the word 'greed'. But I have a question for later about human spirituality that I could tie in with this. Are human beings becoming more spiritual?

The Echo:
Indeed not. There be, indeed, those individuals that do view spirituality as an highly important format within their existences. However in the viewing overall of the planet, these entities be few in relation to the many.

Author:
Could the few not counterbalance the many? Could people who are growing spiritually not raise the so-called vibration of the human race, or of the planet Earth, to a higher level?

The Echo:
Indeed, to some degree. However as prior stated, there be, that refer, greed, uh, avarice, that be strong within those of the physical resonance and those of the physical resonance tend to be also those that be in control format. To maintain a peaceful spirituality may be to invite that of…oh, hmn, hmn physical depredation or death at the hands of those seething with avarice, you understand.

Author:
Going back to the question that we did not finish. What do you see by 2025? Will there be big changes in the weather?

The Echo:

Indeed so. That of the animal man is creating for its environment situations that may not be completely reversible at least within, that refer, lifetimes of those currently in the physical existence.. For here that of the pollutions of the airs, the waters, the lack of regard for the Earth in order to achieve riches or fame can only result in that of, here, another shuddering of the planet. In this manner the planet fights for its natural state, of which man has desecrated a great deal to present. This will cause the planet in its fight to retain its natural state to present windstorms, earth quakes, water risings and indeed, that refer, famine in some lands. And this be an gradual increasing format to that point at which the animal man begins to think, you understand.

Author:
This is a different topic. When people ask questions, you present answers in a matter-of-fact way. You do not seem to speculate or say the way you would like things to be. You tell us the way things are, as you know them. You speak of good things and bad equally without emotion Are you emotionally involved with human development and with what is going on on the planet Earth. Do things make you happy or sad? Or are you immune from these emotions?

The Echo:
Indeed so. Understand we have stated that the animal man is on an course of self-destruction in the physical realm. You understand, this is indeed an fine format, do the entity man choose to do so. For that of the, here, in that refer, the final analysis, free choice reigns supreme. Entities in the physical may do whatever they desire to do, merely because of their ability of free choice, you understand. There be neither right nor wrong here.
And as thee have requested, no we do not become here emotionally involved. Eh for what purpose? It be not of import to we, for we merely move on to another area. Perhap another planetary civilization. It be not of great import to we, do the physical entities choose to destroy selves, you understand.

Author.

OK. But as Linda was saying, we do pick up your love for us. *(Human beings.)* You do have love for us. You don't worry about our planet, but you do have love for us.

The Echo:
Indeed so. You understand, love is all-encompassing and love is non-judgmental. Do an entity state to thee that it love thee and then state to thee that thee be not the type of person that it really wish to associate with, you understand, this is not 'love', this is 'like'.

Author:
OK. You also must realize while we are down here worrying about our lives...and thinking that this illusion is our reality... and even if we did blow up the planet, you must realize that our essence will not be hurt. We will still survive. If our bodies die in a dying planet, our spirits then will go somewhere else. Just as you say you will go somewhere else. Is this correct?

The Echo:
Indeed so.

Author:
So then, it is almost as if we will all get together someday and we will say that we messed that one up. We were good here and we did these things well, but we messed that one up.

The Echo:
Perhap not. Perhap not messed up. Perhap learned an important lesson for each individual in that particular scenario.

Author:
Something tells me that as real as this physical world seems, it must be just a temporary illusion. It is an instrument to teach us and for our growth and learning...because something that looks this beautiful and wonderful...to destroy that and not feel sad about it, then you must realize that this is not an ultimate reality.

The Echo:
Indeed. In your terms of speaking, indeed so. For we understand that do the physical human entities destroy that of their present environment, we do not view this as, in thy terms, an terrible thing, this be merely an occurrence and those entities that have moved into spirit will...hmn ...understanding terms, travel to other experiences.

Author:
(Laughing)
You would make a wonderful parent and a lot of children would love to have you as a parent because it does not sound as if you would be scolding and worrying every minute. You would let the children go out and play and learn.

The Echo:
Indeed so.

Author:
I have a few questions, since we are talking about other worlds and other existences. I have a few questions about ETs. Which countries and governments have had direct contacts with Extra-Terrestrials?

The Echo:
Canada, United States, Mexico, Britain, Norway, Sweden, Germany, France, Spain, Brazil...

Author:
May I interrupt at this point? By a direct contact, I mean Extra-Terrestrials have come to the attention of these governments? Is that correct?

The Echo:
Indeed so.

Author:
OK. I will let you continue with the list.

The Echo:
Uruguay, Argentina, Australia, India, South Africa. The, remainder of, that refer, Africa have been, as it were, turning a blind eye.

Author:
You have not mentioned the Soviet Union, or any Eastern European countries. Or Russia, as the Soviet Union is now called.

The Echo:
Russia. Indeed so. There be here contacts made here within approximately 1930-35.

Author:
So all these governments have had contact with ETs. Were the ETs physically present on the ground in the countries or flying over in the sky? And did they meet government leaders?

The Echo:
Indeed there be here an degree of each of these aspects. The meeting of government leaders... Canada, Britain, United States, France, that refer, Russia...Norway, Sweden.

Author:
So, obviously the government leaders have decided not to reveal this to the public. Can you tell us their motivation? Why are they keeping this private or secret?

The Echo:
Be partially the maintenance of non-panic situations. It be also that of the maintenance of the religions of the lands, for this would destroy the religions and thus create degree, that refer, anarchy within the lands. Also it behoove governments that the informations be maintained secretly for there be here dealings with these entities. The agreement to accept technological learnings and in return to allow that of physical examinations of some physical entities of the planet Earth.

Author:
Do you agree with the assessment that if this were made known, there would be anarchy? Do you think that is most likely?

The Echo:
Indeed so. That of the general populace would become, oh here in thy colloquial terms, chickens without heads, you understand.

Author:
I believe you have said, in another session in the past, that the presence of ETs will be made known. Did you say by 2006 or 2007?

The Echo:
Indeed. Within that, oh, here refer, rough time span. Indeed so.

Author:
So within two years we can expect some government in the world to announce to its population that they have had contact with creatures from outside the planet Earth?

The Echo:
Indeed so.

Author:
Why will they be making that announcement?

The Echo:
It be that of the decision to, as it were, be honest in approach to the publics and...uh...will find that there be great derision and opposition to this format. Uh...be then, oh, as it were, lessening of discussion.

Author:
Has there not also been pressure from citizens, who believe that there have always been Extra-Terrestrials here, to get this information from governments, too?

The Echo:
Indeed so. Understand, however, that refer the... oh... freedom of information acts be...oh... somewhat open to translation and this be the freedom of information to that which we feel you should receive, you understand.

Author:
Linda once asked, when I was at an Echo session, about the men in black. You answered that there are men in black. These are ETs. Could you explain that? Are they mixing in human society? Have they taken on the appearance of human beings?

The Echo:
These entities may be here referred watchers. Be working under the auspices of, that refer, the governmental authority. The attempt to maintain the secrecy of the occurrences that be about.

Author:
Are men in black some human beings...some government agents, and some ETs? And they would all appear to us as human beings?

The Echo:
Indeed so.

Author:
How do they manage this? Do they look the way we do, or is it some kind of illusion? How do they look like us, to us?

The Echo:
Hmn... in the simplest of understanding terms, makeup.

Author:
(Laughter)
How do you take a little green man and turn him into a six-foot tall...?

The Echo:
We did not say little green man.

Author:
Then we are dealing with races or species who are fairly close to human beings in their appearance.

The Echo:
Indeed. Humanoid in nature.

Author:
Humanoid. Interesting. Or we could look at it another way and say that human beings are just one branch of humanoid creatures.

The Echo:
Indeed so. You understand the human animal have been, as it were, transplanted upon the planet Earth.

Author:
Sometimes your answers are so…I don't know…so overwhelming. I am like Linda when she said that she was speechless once from the answers she received.
(Laughing)
A lot of questions but I want to absorb the information.

The Echo:
We find that speechless part difficult to believe.

Author:
Would you believe if I am speechless for five seconds?

The Echo:
Hmn. Perhap.

(Laughter)

Author:
OK. Maybe the wheels in my mind are turning more quickly than the words will come out. I want to think about the answers

more than I want to ask additional questions. Maybe that is what I mean. This has been very good information today.

Chapter 5
The Spirit realm, God, humanity's past and future

November 25, 2005
St. Catharines, Ontario

Present: Cliff Preston, channeling The Echo
  Linda Preston, directing the session
  Author, asking questions for this book.

Author:
What is it like where The Echo are?
Could you describe your existence?
What you do...anything you could tell us about your dimension.

The Echo:
Indeed. We will state to thee... it be limitless in relation to spacial orientation. In relation to physical orientation, there be not, you understand.
It be much as a droplet of water floating somewhere in a vast ocean, you understand. And of occasion there be an sense of a calling, of a need, and those in the, refer, spirit realm, be drawn to the calling. The calling be from physical entities and the spiritual entities then move to assist. There be not, here that refer, vision as thee know vision of the eyes. There be some degree of vision of the senses, vision of the mind. However, to explain this in terms of physical Earth inhabitants, is of extreme difficulty, you understand.
For those in the physical realm have not a frame of reference in which to understand. There be...suffice to say...there be an

limitless expanse, that in which any and all spirits be alone, you understand. Yet at once and the same time, there be limitless numbers of spirits about. They do not be viewed each by the other unless by request of one or another, you understand.

Author:
It is interesting that when I asked the question, you gave an answer in reference to a physical space...and your saying there is a lack of space. But you did not say that we are blissful, we are peaceful, we are wise or...

The Echo:
Indeed we are not, you understand. To state of any entity in the spirit realm, it is much, much as it were within the physical realm. To assume that because an entity has moved into spirit, it has suddenly become wise and wonderful and all-knowing is to give far too much credence to each individual entity. The purpose of the incarnational and reincarnational evolution of an entity is to grow, to develop, to eventually return to that which is then termed, in thy understanding, the Godhead, you understand. Therefore, an entity in the spirit realm may not be greatly different from the time, as you know time, when it was in the physical realm. Merely have, here refer, larger comparative overview of the physical perception.

Linda:
Echo, would you change Cliff's position?

The Echo:
You understand ah, to state ah hmn that the, here refer, hmnn...the great archangel is assisting one in the physical realm is indeed an ohm hmn pleasant and wondrous solution for those in the physical realm. However, you understand that which may be termed, here example, Archangel Michael, this indeed may be, that refer here, in they terms, Uncle Harry, you understand. For that of the term, Archangel Michael, is an oh hmn is a physical realm description of an unknown entity, you understand.

Author:
You have more control now. You have... as you say you can...There is limitless space, you understand more than you did on Earth, you have control of your being, your mental powers, is that correct?

The Echo:
Indeed to some degree.

Author:
Is there not an active presence of God where you are? Or a part of God which is external to you?

The Echo:
Indeed. We have not seen it.

Author:
Could you talk about the possibility?

The Echo:
Indeed, not.

Author:
OK.

Linda:
Would you explain what God is? You have explained this before.

The Echo:
Within that of the understanding of the entities in the physical realm, indeed so. It be that of the...oh...forces, the powers, the activities of the universe that...hmn...activate, that refer, humanity, you understand. That of the force that be termed God, is indeed that - a force. It is an energy, oh...that is inherent in all individuals, be they physical or be they spiritual. And be not of that an, here refer, oooh...overseeing, all-powerful entity, you understand. That of the force, refer, God have been so named merely for identification. There be not an explanation presently

available to those in the physical realm for that which thee refer God. It be the unknown force that saturates all within thy universe.

Linda:
Echo, in June 1980, before Cliff and I got together, I had a dream in which I filled the entire universe. I did not feel alone. I was just aware of filling the entire universe. Is this what you were describing?

The Echo:
Indeed so. It be that of the, here refer, life force energies of the universe.

Author:
Some religions believe that we on Earth can help spirits. Is there anything that we can do to help spirits?

The Echo:
Indeed so. Do spirits require assistance, indeed so.

Author:

(Laughing)

I don't think that many of us would know when a spirit was asking for help. You once said that there is no point in praying for the souls in purgatory, kind of thing.

The Echo:
Indeed, we do not view, that refer, purgatory.

Author:
However, what if we were to send you our love. Would that do any good for you?

The Echo:
We would indeed love thee. We would indeed receive this well.

Author:
So if we were to have an idea in our minds that we were going to send love... *last words not recorded as tape runs out.*

Tape turned over.

Author:
You once said that Cliff Preston was a channeler named Montmorency in a past life in France.
Could you comment on any other lives in which he was a channeler?

The Echo:
Indeed be in performance of channeling in the form of Montmorency in that of the land France. This be, of approximate year, 1640 and the entity be set upon by, that refer, church, declared a heretic, and be sentenced to demise. This occur through the format of garrote and fire, you understand.
The entity have performed in the format channeling, you understand, in thy understanding uh channeling be a recent term usage, in thy time understanding. Beyond this be that of a deep trance psychic or that of mesmerized individual, you understand, taken from the word Mesmer. The entity have performed this format in that of the, refer oh, land Canada of approximate year 1915 and here the entity be in advisement to that of, here refer, military...oh...officers in order to discover what, that refer, the enemy of the military is about to perform. This be in thy terms world war, you understand.

Linda:
What would his name have been?

The Echo:
Albert ...Albert hmmnn unclear...Keefer or Quinn such as.

Linda:
Is that when he crossed over in 1915?

The Echo:
In 1917 the entity crossed, in that of the area, here refer, eastern portion of that land refer France.

Linda:
Where was his home in Canada?

The Echo:
Indeed. Strongest, strongest draw here be that of the westerly…refer, Calgary.

Linda:
With the name that you gave, would we be able to locate…

The Echo:
High degree probability.

Linda:
Was the Quinn that I knew in Cold Lake…Was she related to Cliff?

The Echo:
Year of connection?

Linda:
1962-63-64. She was a nurse there.

The Echo:
Indeed the entity be, as it were, a distant relation of that of the form Clifford. That be in the present existence of the form Clifford.

Linda:
Is it possible because of the name Quinn that you are mentioning, or similar to that, would it be that line of…

The Echo:
High degree probability, indeed so.

Linda:
So if he went back to his time line, would his name show on that? Because he got that from his uncle last year.

The Echo:
That refer family tree?

Linda:
Yes.

The Echo:
Indeed be that of the, here refer, that of the parents indeed so. However, that of the offspring of the parents be somewhat misplaced.

Linda:
So Albert may not be on there then, is that correct ?

The Echo:
Indeed there do be that refer Albert, however be approx 1940s.

Linda:
So not the same Albert Quinn?

The Echo:
Indeed not.

Linda:
And that name would not be on...

The Echo:
High degree improbability.

Linda:
OK. Are you drawn to the name of his parents at that time... would that be there? Or children?

The Echo:
Indeed William be strongest.

Linda:
OK William Quinn would that have been his father?

The Echo:
High degree probability.

Author:
Echo, does Cliff Preston in this lifetime have any connection with Edgar Cayce, now or in previous lifetimes?

The Echo:
Indeed. There do be, that refer, encounters. However in relation to that refer connection, we would assume that thee mean a personal connection. Indeed not. The form of the one Clifford hearing of, that refer, entity Cayce of approximately year 1941...the entity Clifford immediately understood at that age of 6 or 7 years exactly that which is being performed by this entity Cayce, you understand.. There be a mental connection and there be not that of the physical connection.

Author:
When he heard about Edgar Cayce he understood what was going on? Even though Cliff was a child?

The Echo:
Indeed so.

Author:
I think in the past though you suggested there was some kind of connection. An aspect or an element of the Edgar Cayce personality has reincarnated in the form of Clifford Preston?

The Echo:
Indeed. Have indeed joined with we, indeed so.

Author:
Oh. I understand. Part of The Echo.

The Echo:
Indeed so. You understand this is an entirely different query.
Be that of the, here refer, soul energies of the entity have indeed been drawn somewhat to assist along with that we refer The Echo.

Author:
Soul energies of the form who was Edgar Cayce are now assisting The Echo. That would be useful because he has been on both sides now. He has been on the Earth side receiving messages and now he is on the other side helping to give us messages.

The Echo:
Indeed.

Author:
That is interesting.

Linda:
So he is not in the physical now? Is that what you are saying Echo?

The Echo:
We did not say this.

(Laughter)

Author:
I think they are saying that when Edgar Cayce died some soul energies have remained on the spiritual side to help and other soul energies have now reincarnated. Because at one time you told me that there is a woman in California who does psychic work and you said she is the reincarnation of Edgar Cayce.

The Echo:
Indeed so. You understand, it be that of an strong energy resonance with this entity, indeed so.

Author:
The living psychic in California today has a strong energy resonance of Edgar Cayce?

The Echo:
Indeed so.

Linda:
Is this the…

Author:
Not Sylvia Browne. I think Echo once suggested the initials JC…

The Echo:
High degree probability.

Author:
I am getting the impression that all of the energy in a human being may not necessarily ever stay together. If I were to go into the spirit realm, my energies then could go in different directions. And that collection of energy may not be in one place or a physical body again. Is that correct?

The Echo:
Indeed so. You understand that which be viewed in the physical realm as ghosts, this be an real viewing by physical entity how it be merely an portion of the entities that have created those actions. You understand the ghost is merely that of an resonance of an entity gone by.

Author:
I would also like to include in the book , some other things that will draw a reader's attention and give a reader something to think about. So could you comment on Sai Baba?

The Echo:
Indeed. The entity refer to Sathya Sai Baba?

Author:
Yes. In India.

The Echo:
This entity be of, here refer, high degree of, that refer, spiritual energy. The entity understand at an young physical age the workings, as it were, the working of the universe. And in so understanding the entity have attempted to show others in the physical realm that their perception is of extreme limitation. The entity have attempted to show those in the physical realm that it is entirely possible for they to enter into totality of control of their own life patterns, their own environment merely through the understanding of the workings of the universe. In an attempt to show these entities, Sai Baba have performed those actions which be termed by, here refer, comparative less-aware individuals to be miracles, you understand. They be not miracles. They be merely the use of the energies of the universe. And that of the form Sai Baba will be the first individual to state to one that he is no different than any other. He merely understands the workings of the universe.

Author:
What can you tell us about allegations of misconduct. I believe that some persons become followers for a while and then they leave disenchanted. They say various things. What can you tell us about that?

The Echo:
Indeed so. We state to thee in thy colloquial terms "sour grapes." The entities tend to be drawn to those that understand the powers of the universe. These entities then expect that the, here refer, the avatar will do for them, you understand. When this does not occur, when the avatar does not meet the expectations of these entities, it is then spoken about in derision. You understand, this be due to the expectations being unmet and, that refer, Sai Baba will not meet expectations. An law of the universe is that expectations are seldom met, you understand.

Author:

So the sour grapes would be such things as allegations of sexual misconduct and all that kind of thing?

The Echo:
Indeed so. Kind, loving entities that approach with smiles and great expectations, upon losing their expectations or their sense of wonder and awe, then, indeed will speak in negative terms, in relation to the avatar in order to justify their own beings for their withdrawal or failure to understand.

Linda:
Echo, for the past few years I have been hearing what he is referring to...how many believe this?

The Echo:
It matter not.

Linda:
I know it doesn't matter, but I am curious. How many believe this?

The Echo:
Indeed, you understand, there will always be those within the physical realm willing to believe the worst of anyone. You understand there be those presently within thy environs that believe that thee and the form Clifford are of evil format.

Linda:
Yes. My family.

The Echo:
Indeed so. Therefore understand, it matter not. You understand, would the starving children refuse the food that is offered by an entity because they thought that entity did not maintain their beliefs?

Author:
OK. Echo, a number of years ago during an Echo session, when you were briefly mentioning Sai Babba...I might have been

asking about avatars or people with enlightened consciousness or heightened awareness…you said there is also an avatar in Africa, that you mentioned after you mentioned Sai Babba. Could you tell us about this other person?

The Echo:
Indeed, there be very little may be stated about this other. This entity remain quietly, as it were, aloof from the world, merely working its energies in quietude without fanfare. Have encountered that of the form, Sai Babba at one point in its existence. The form Sai Babba travel to the, as it were, jungles of Central Africa to meet with this avatar and these entities form a bond that is designed to begin to alter the consciousness of the continent Africa and indeed of all peoples.

Linda:
Echo, I have been a little curious. Did he want everybody to know that there is another avatar on this planet and that is why he did it that way? Because the way he can…he can travel instantly to somewhere else.

The Echo:
It be deemed necessary, understand, that it be known others maintain the same understanding or similar understanding of the universal energy. It be merely that of the major populations of the planet be in involvement of daily existence and the acceptance of rules and regulations from political leaders and religious leaders and therefore be of extreme limitation in their thought processes.

Linda:
Trying to teach everybody that they are truly equal. Merely opening up ourselves to accept that there is more. Everybody sees him as mother-father and I see him as brother-sister. So which is correct?

The Echo:

Indeed. Both. You understand thee speak of male entity, female entity and, understand, this occur only within the physical realm. Within the spirit realm be that refer sexless, you understand.

Author:
We will leave the avatar in Africa and I will ask you about somebody else.

We read this week in the paper a number of articles about a 15-year-old Nepalese named Ram Bahadur Banjan. According to his followers he has been meditating for 6 months. Could you tell us anything about him?

The Echo:
Indeed. You understand. This entity have be born into the physical realm as that which is in thy society, here uhm...mmnnn...we lose the term, be born that refer gifted offspring, you understand. Be born as an old entity as opposed to an baby offspring. The mind of the entity be clear and concise . Have be noticed by parents, by those in the spiritual practices at an early age and the entity have been tutored, learning the methods of deep meditations and have indeed entered into, that refer, long-term meditative state. However, this is not of a continuous state. This entity enter into meditation at, that refer, at sunrise and withdraw of the meditations approximately sunset of each and every day. The entity do indeed require water and do indeed require that refer standard sleep format and this entity then rise and enter into meditative depth at sunrise and carry forth to beyond sunset each and every day. This is due to the trainings of the entity. And do indeed be, as it were, touted as that of the reincarnation of Buddha for this will draw many entities of curiosity and spiritual want. However, we view this entity as of high degree spirituality, of high degree purpose and be not that refer Buddha. It be of here 1200-1400 prior physical associations. However it be not, that refer, Buddha, you understand.

Author:

Before the session, Linda held up the newspaper article and without looking at the front of the clipping, she said she felt a lot of love.

Linda:
No, I had to look at the picture.

Author:
Oh, OK.

The Echo:
Indeed so. This indeed be a strong format within the entity, you understand. This entity also have desire to show its capabilities to its people but its people do live in a highly physically oriented society and the entity have in its purpose the strong desire to show to its people that through the use of quietude, the use of love and the control of thy own personal environment, greater comparative levels of existence can be achieved.

Linda:
I had a hard time breathing too, as if there were something in the lungs.

The Echo:
Indeed, this be due to that of the, as it were, slowing of the hmnn…respiratory actions of the physical body through the use of the mind. The entity at the ending of its day beyond sunset must needs then clear its lungs daily.

Author:
So Linda's impressions were correct. Linda was sensitive to certain aspects about this.

The Echo:
Indeed so.

Author:

OK. You are saying there is value in this but other persons may ask what he is accomplishing, if he is just sitting there meditating. Could you explain the value of what he is doing?

The Echo:
Indeed. That of the value is to show others the possibilities for selves, you understand. The entity will, with highest probability, will not make a great difference to a great number of individuals. However, the entity will make a great difference to a small number of individuals and this is an beginning, you understand.

Author:
Is there some unfortunate thing developing around this? Maybe his followers...

Several words not recorded as first tape ends and a second tape begins

Tape 2.

The Echo:
...that in its mind, there do be an degree of the, that here refer, cataloging or categorizing of individuals, and it is a truism that like individuals experience like occurrences within their physical experience, you understand. And this be known deeply within.

Linda:
...because of what I was experiencing...things like how people looked...and this is what I have also brought to this present life. So what I have experienced in the past on how people are, when they look in certain ways.

The Echo:
Indeed. We could not say it better.

Author:
That was interesting. I did want to make more of the fact that Linda is that sensitive. She picked up the article and she just

looked at it, without reading it, and she had those impressions. The impression of great love for people and also she picked up…not… she did not just say that this boy is having trouble breathing, Linda had experienced a sympathetic reaction, she had a bit of trouble breathing…(*To Linda*) yourself?

Linda:
Yes.

Author:
Yes, that is correct. So for Linda to pick up that much…she could feel the love, she did not just say that this man or this boy has love, I think she felt love and she also physically felt the breathing.

Would you comment again on Linda's abilities?

The Echo:
Indeed. You understand, the form of the one Linda understand that all in the universe be in connection, each of the other. To merely, as it were, to look at an picture of an individual is, indeed, to contact the energy of that individual and in so doing the form of the one Linda through its practice, learning, training, can then feel within its own physical body the resonances of that individual, you understand.

Author:
So Linda is still growing and progressing. She is developing from the illness that she had a number of years ago. She is leaving that illness in the past, now.

The Echo:
Indeed, so.

Author:
That's good.

(To Linda) I was quite impressed. That is the reason that I handed you the article when I came in. To see what impression you had.

Linda:
Would you mind changing Cliff's position again?

The Echo:
We are ahead of thee.

(Laughter)

Linda:
You did that and I was not watching. I apologize.

Author:
Next area is a little off this topic.
I have been reading about people being under psychic attack and a person sending another person bad thoughts. Wishing bad things for others. The idea of picking up negativity from the atmosphere around you. Would you explain how a person could develop a spiritual protection for...say...himself and for loved ones?

The Echo:
Indeed. Primary step is to remove fear. You understand. To understand that no other individual can affect thee in any manner unless thee agree to that. Agreement can take the form of fear or the understanding that the other individual is more powerful than self. Here the primary step then be to understand that all entities in the physical realm and the spiritual realm be operating on an oh, here refer, in thy colloquial terms, on an level table top. You understand. Equal. Equal. Equal. And if an entity direct negativity towards one it is necessary only to reject negativity. Replace that negativity with positivity. Oh, and in an extreme case to surround self within that of which be, refer here, the white light of the universe, which is indeed the positivity that is emanated from thy own mind, you understand. Create about thee an bubble of protective white light that allow

only positivity into thy being. And this is a simple matter. It be not of difficulty in any form. And those that be presenting to thee the negativity cannot, cannot penetrate if this be maintained.

Author:
I think you would agree that we probably could hurt ourselves with our own minds more than another person could hurt us.

The Echo:
Indeed so. Those in the physical realm do this a number of times daily, you understand.

Author:
With worry and repeating the negative thoughts about ourselves.

The Echo:
Indeed so. And within thy society such as: "Oh, I know even if I go to that job interview, I am not going to get the job." Indeed, then thee will not get the job, for thee have already stated the outcome.

Author:
A mind should come with…

Linda:
That way they won't be disappointed, you see.

Author:
Yes.
A mind should come with a warning label saying: "Caution must use very carefully."

(Laughter)

The Echo:
Indeed. Unfortunately, there is no handbook, you understand.

Author:
True.

The Echo:
Thee are offered the opportunity to enter into the physical realm...eh...to learn, to grow, to develop, in whichever manner thee do so desire. For that refer, ehm...uhm, free choice is always reign supreme, you understand. An entity may use its life pattern in an positive manner or an negative manner, whichever it so choose to learn and develop. That of right and wrong be an oh human concept, you understand.

Author:
Over the years, I am seeing more and more, things that I am reading and discussing with others, I am seeing more and more that the idea of life being a very structured thing and everything thought out down to the last detail is not true because it just seems so much freer, and unstructured and open, and it can do what it wants.

The Echo:
Indeed so. And change, you understand, change is the only constant in the universe.

Author:
OK. I would like to ask about a couple of things that are controversial. Could you tell us about the Philadelphia Experiment. It was 1943. The USS Eldridge. I believe it was in the harbour. Could you tell us what happened?

The Echo:
Indeed. This be the instigating of, that refer, cloaking device. However, that which in actuality occurred, be that the cloaking device caused that of, here refer, hmn...alternate reality gateway and the, oh, Eldridge and all of its seamen were transported to an alternate reality, and then returned. And this be an, as it were, complete disassemblement of the molecules of steel and of human bodies and the, oh, upon the return uh due to the, here refer, movement of the human bodies, uh...some human bodies became embedded within the structures of the ship, you

understand. This be due to an unknown error in calculations and have since been only used in very small applications.

Linda:
Small applications? What are you referring to that is now a small application?

The Echo:
Indeed. That refer cloaking device of such as, that refer stealth fighter.

Author:
This sounds so amazing that it takes me back to my earlier question. That... now...this is another example of how fluid reality is, how fluid things can be, unstructured. Because a logical mind would say that this could not be. And maybe a religious person would say: "Oh that could not have happened because God would not allow that to happen." Or even if you say a life force would not allow that to happen.
So could you explain why there is no overall controlling force that could keep that from happening and how could people fooling around with an experiment, actually cause something like that to happen?

The Echo:
Indeed. You understand. Firstly, as prior stated, that of free choice reign supreme. That of the, that which be referred, the God energy will not, cannot intervene in any form. That of those entities in experimentation, come to the understanding of that of the fluidity, indeed, of, refer, physical universe. However the entities do not have, here refer, control over all aspects of that fluidity. These entities merely understand that nothing...nothing on the planet is solid. In reality, you understand, and in so understanding they generate an means of...uhm...breaking down the molecular structure to create totality of fluidity, and indeed, this, as it were in thy terms, backfire.

Author:

One would also be quite amazed to think that the technology we have in the year 2005 compared to 1943 is much more advanced. So it is truly amazing that someone could actually have caused this to happen, whether it was by plan or miscalculation. Someone in 1943. That technology they had was quite advanced, was it not?

The Echo:
Indeed so.
However, in comparison be not nearly as advanced as that of, approximate here, 70-80,000 years in that which thee refer past.

Author:
Ah. OK. I see.
Another thing. The Philadelphia Experiment is connected to the Montauk Project on Long Island, New York.

The Echo:
Indeed. That of the, here refer, Montauk Project be the residue of, that refer, Philadelphia Experiment.

Author:
Residue. Do you mean...?

The Echo:
That of the Philadelphia Experiment be technically abandoned and the Montauk be, as it were, constructed in order to continue investigations in this aspect.

Linda:
Echo, what we saw in the movie with the other reality in the 1980s, and this was affected by what happened in 1943, is that true? Or was that just a story?

The Echo:
Indeed. This be fabrication.

Linda:
OK. I was curious.

Author:
It was good entertainment though.
Then the Montauk Project...you were saying that the cloaking device technology has been used only occasionally, I think you said, since 1943. This is one of the examples of when it was used.
Are you saying that in the 1970s, when the Montauk Project was active, they decided to use the Philadelphia Experiment technology again, or somehow from the past (the Philadelphia Experiment technology) caused the Montauk Project to happen?

The Echo:
Indeed. It be merely that of the re-investigation, however of an, refer, comparative more secret manner, you understand. This also be in strong resonance of, that refer, Groom Lake, of North America.

Linda:
Echo, this is part of what my brother experienced in Trenton? Was it the US government in Trenton?

The Echo:
Indeed not. It be that of the Canadian government.

Linda:
OK. And that's where they did that worst driving test outside the regular base?

The Echo:
Indeed so.

Linda:
And because of what my brother had experienced in Trenton, is that why nobody was allowed to go to that old base?

The Echo:
Indeed so. You understand, the village, the town of Montauk be terrorized by the energy forms moving about its town.

Linda:
So it was not just my brother who experienced that?

The Echo:
Indeed not.

Author:
Where is Groom Lake again?

The Echo:
Indeed this be that refer Area 51.

Author:
Oh yes.
So they were experimenting with a cloaking device and they were able to manipulate or use the fluidity of all things. Is there also time travel involved?

The Echo:
Indeed there have been that of effort of, that refer, time travel. However, there have been, that refer, lost individuals and this be presently avoided.

Linda:
This thing in Trenton, you said Canadian, but were they also co-operating with the U.S?

The Echo:
Indeed so.

Linda:
OK. So they were doing testing in more than one area, then.

The Echo:
Indeed, so , several areas.

Linda:
Would you mind commenting on what places they were?

The Echo:
There be locations central Ohio, Nevada, California, Florida.

Linda:
Are you drawn to the names?

The Echo:
Indeed not of present.

Linda:
If we checked into it, would we be able to locate these towns?

The Echo:
High degree probability.

Linda:
So this is the only place in Canada?

The Echo:
We did not say this.

Linda:
I am asking.

The Echo:
Indeed. There be experiments at , that refer, Borden, at refer Shilo, at, refer, Cold Lake.

Linda:
Is that one of the weird experiences I had there at Cold Lake? Because of that?

The Echo:
Indeed, so.

Author:
Cold Lake? Is that Alberta?

Linda:
Yes. An air force base.
What province is Shilo?

The Echo:
Manitoba, that refer Brandon.

Linda:
OK.

The Echo:
Form of Cifford gaining somewhat in rigidity.

Linda:
OK, then Echo, would you mind putting Cliff back in the position he was in when he started?.

Cliff's form returns to upright position.

Linda:
Thank you for this session.

The Echo:
Indeed. We of The Echo thank thee of the opportunity of approach. Therefore we say go in love, peace and understanding.

Tape turned off and back on.

Cliff's impression:
"Towers, and wires, water beside it. Lake or ocean can't tell. Looked like a power station."

Chapter 6 Roswell, Shag Harbour, ETs

February 6, 2006
St. Catharines, Ontario

Present: Cliff Preston, channeling The Echo
          Linda Preston, directing the session
          Author, asking questions for this book.

Author:
I would like to ask you what happened in Roswell, New Mexico in 1947?

The Echo:
Indeed. That refer, discombobulation of, that refer, operators of space vehicle resulting...uh, also due to that of environmental disruption...thunderstorm uh, also create difficulty here and the entities crash, you understand.

Author:
Who were these entities?

The Echo:
Be that of crew of four Grays.

Author:
Large or small?

The Echo:
Indeed. This be an comparative format. These entities all be the same size.

Author:
But I think there is a categorization for large Grays and small Grays.

The Echo:
Indeed so. We would state here small.

Author:
Small. So there was a crash. Four Grays were killed...and the United States government, I guess first of all through the air force....

The Echo:
Three Grays were killed.

Author:
What happened to the fourth?

The Echo:
The fourth was, as it were, taken and examined and later enter into demise.

Author:
A natural death?

The Echo:
Indeed not. It be due to lack of sufficient nutritions for this entity and lack of sufficient environment...um, here refer... suffice to say sufficient of air.

Author:
So there has been a coverup, ever since, by the United Sates air force and United States government?

The Echo:
Indeed so. Uh, these entities have taken upon selves as that which they view as the safety of the nation. These entities then feel that to allow the general populace to be in knowledge that there do indeed be other peoples, other creatures, other modes of travel in the universe beyond that which is known upon the planet Earth is to create panic and to create great difficulties within that of the religious structures of all major religions within that of the planet Earth. These entities then enter into decision of the totality of secrecy forever.

Author:
You mean the American authorities have entered into that decision?

The Echo:
Indeed so.

Author:
What about the Grays? Have they suggested that the American authorities keep it secret or do they care if it is made known to the public?

The Echo:
Hmn, indeed. These entities have entered into discussions and do, indeed, wish that the general public be in full knowledge of they. Highest probability there be further informations available... uh, approximate July, August of the year present.

Author:
You are saying that the United States government may make some information about Roswell public in July or August of this year, 2006?

The Echo:
Indeed not. We did not say this. We said that there be further informations made available to the general public by, that refer, the Grays.

Author:
Ah hah.

Linda:
How will it be made known?

The Echo:
High degree probability visual in nature.

Linda:
In what area or areas?

The Echo:
Indeed. Be a number of areas. Be that of, here refer, several locations within, that refer, North America. There be a location be within that of an, approximate here, 20-30 mile radius of thy present location.

Linda:
Of this area?

The Echo:
Indeed so. There be locations that of Sweden, Norway, France, Germany, Austria and of the African continent.

Author:
OK. I would like to relate that to an incident at Shag Harbour, Nova Scotia, on October 4, 1967. This is believed to be an extra-terrestrial space craft also.

The Echo:
Indeed. Penetrating the waters of the bay. Indeed.

Author:
Could you briefly describe to us what happened in that incident?

The Echo:
Indeed. Vehicle penetrate the waters of the bay, enter beneath the waters of the bay, and appear to those… oh… those viewing …it appear as a crash. However it be not, that refer, crash it be merely the penetrating of these waters, the entity then…oh, oh…move the vehicle beneath the surface of the ocean out into, that refer, the North Atlantic ocean.

Linda:
Echo, you told M. that he would also be seeing ETs this year. Is this the one …when you said within 20-30 miles within the St.Catharines area?

The Echo:
Indeed so.

Author:
OK. Why did this vehicle go below the surface of the water? Why did it go so close to shore? Did the occupants know that it would be seen by some people?

The Echo:
Indeed not. It be merely a decision that it move beneath the surface for it have, oh here refer, gener...regeneration that is required...eh through the use of water and it be merely, here refer, be not in concern of those that may view it. It merely enter.

Author:
The ship needed to go under the surface of the ocean to use the ocean water to regenerate itself...as a fuel system or something like that?

The Echo:
Indeed so.

Author:
Interesting. And then it probably just rose above the surface of the ocean and left the Earth?

The Echo:
Indeed so.

Author:
They don't have a base under the ocean?

The Echo:
Be not in that particular area.

Author:
There is a base?

The Echo:
Within that of the North Atlantic, indeed so. Southeasterly of, that refer, the southerly tip of, that refer, Greenland.

Author:
Were they the Grays again?

The Echo:
Indeed so.

Author:
They are getting to be our favorite ETs.

(Laughter)

The Echo:
Be that refer most common, most prominent about that of the planet Earth.

Linda:
Echo, what I have experienced. I have mentioned this. I guess it was 1979. When I went out of body, I saw ETs and I felt that…they were robotic…

The Echo:
Indeed. Robotic.

Linda:
Are they the same people that would be in contact?

The Echo:
Uh, some. Indeed so. You understand, do not, here refer, draw lines, in that of the use of some vehicles, it indeed be robotic in nature, in that of the use of some vehicles it be humanoid in nature.

Author:
Are the Grays Arcturians? The Arcturians, you have said, are the predecessors of human beings on Earth.

The Echo:
In thy terms of understanding of Arcturius, indeed so.

Author:
So the Grays are our forefathers and foremothers? (Laughing)

The Echo:
Indeed. The great grandmummy and granddaddy.

Author:
Great grandmummy and granddaddy. And there is a family resemblance? (Laughing)

The Echo:
To some degree. Indeed so.

Author:
This is an odd idea though. (Outcasts sent to Earth) Apart from whether I believe it. Because to put it all in the context of Earth.... England used to send prisoners to Australia at one time. The prisoners realized that they were sent out and had a connection with the English. In fact, today some Australians are proud that they were rebellious and independent. In this case, you have said that Earth was colonized... and then they forget about us or do not want us to know that they colonized us?

The Echo:
Indeed. It be not a matter of forgetting, you understand. It be a matter of determining that those placed upon the planet Earth in that of an approximate 35-45,000 years prior of present...that these entities must needs to develop for self in their own manner, for these entities lack that of the, here refer, green of the auras and this create for these entities that of an antisocial activities in their home environment. The entities then be, as it were, eh transported to the planet Earth, set upon the planet Earth, and allowed to grow and develop in whichever manner they do so choose, you understand.

Linda:

I am a little confused. When you say 35-45,000 years ago. I thought the people who had come to this planet at that time came here to help those...but the way you are talking...

The Echo:
Indeed not. You understand. There do be some entities that indeed be placed along with the, refer here, castoffs in order to assist with knowledges, to maintain the abilities of the mind, to assist these entities to grow, if they desire, you understand. We have stated to thee, entities such as thy fabled magician Merlin, you understand, have had the abilities, the knowledges available to they to assist. While others at the same time and social environs be not in these knowledges and the, here refer, wizards may then assist they, if assistance is desired and also some of the wizards be set upon by those of less, here refer, less thought distinction and oftime be sent to demise.

Linda:
Echo, when you are talking about green auras...before my illness...when I saw different shades of green, beautiful green, I thought that they were healers, but those who had *(word not clear)* green, I saw them as negative.

The Echo:
You understand. Thee are placing here import upon our words about the green aura of 35-45,000 years prior to, that refer, present. The greens, the colors that thee viewed, be firstly viewed through thy own aura, and secondly be viewed at a point...in time as we know...35-45,000 of years, in thy linear understanding, later. It be not the same in the present as in, that refer, past.

Linda:
OK. So what shade of green are you referring to?

The Echo:
Indeed. Green. You understand. That of the green of these entities be viewed at the time of their removal to the planet Earth. In that of the present, the entities be not the same, you

understand, and the definitions of thy colors be not the same. Therefore, here, do not attempt to place upon the viewing of an aura the translations of which thee be presently aware, for these have not of bearing to, that refer, past.

Linda:
I don't really understand.

The Echo:
Indeed so. Accept that it be different.

Author:
Could I ask another question about something that you mentioned before? I want to put into it into this context. The great power failure in northeastern North America, on November 9th, 1965. You have said that an ET craft was hovering above a power station, I believe somewhere in New York State...

The Echo:
Indeed so.

Author:
...and it needed the power for the ship, so it drained the power from the power plant and it left northeastern North America in darkness for a few days.

The Echo:
Indeed. Caused that of the, refer, electrical equipment to suddenly misfunction.

Author:
Could you talk about that? Was it the Grays in a space ship who wanted power?

The Echo:
Indeed, this be that of, here refer, regeneration also of the energies of the vehicle, indeed so. It be not here viewed, that refer, Grays. In thy terms it be that of the, refer, lizard-type individual that, be here, charge vehicle. This vehicle be of, here

refer, in thy understandings of size...this vehicle be of an approximate 22 miles in circumference, you understand, and this vehicle require a great deal of, that refer, electrical energies both static and active. The entities merely draw from that of high-production power plant upon the planet Earth and use this energies for their revitalization. In so doing, this cause malfunction of electrical transmission equipment on the planet Earth.

Author:
They did not pay for that power. (Laughing)

The Echo:
Hhmmn. You understand...

Author:
We have to pay for power.

The Echo:
You understand, the only persons that pay for power are those that use it secondarily, you understand.

Author:
Could you tell us the name or location of the power plant?

The Echo:
Uh name be not of availability, however, it be of, that refer, the Upper Hudson area.

Author:
I believe you said a policeman did see this spaceship?

The Echo:
Indeed, so. It be summarily discounted.

Author:
I would like to ask a question about the moon. There are theories that the moon is a different age from the Earth. The moon was

brought to its orbit outside the Earth. And that there is an alien base on the moon, an ET base.

The Echo:
Hhmmn indeed. Is presently understood by that of, here refer, research scientific community of the planet Earth that of the moon is of near total different structure from that of the planet Earth. That the moon have many, many, many times, struck by other celestial bodies and this have caused this object to travel through space until it is, as it were...oh, captured by that of the ...oh, gravitational pull of the planet Earth. In this manner that of the moon have remained attached to the planet Earth and exert also its gravitational pull upon the planet. This be in occurrence... oh, in thy terms of understanding, millennia, in that refer years. Far, far beyond the development of...oh, life forms upon that of the planet Earth.

Author:
Could you tell us if there is an alien base or...

The Echo:
Hmn. Yep.

Linda laughs.

Author:
...on the dark side of the moon. There is a base?

The Echo:
Indeed so. You understand that of the refer moon is nonrotational, you understand, and that of the astronauts, the American astronauts, that explore the moon have indeed viewed that of the, here refer, ET base, understand. The entities have indeed radioed to the Earth...uh with the statement of, "Why do they need us here when they have equipment like this? We are like toddlers in baby carriages."

Linda:
It is in that book.

Author:
Yes. Linda has spoken about the book before, Alternative Three, which apparently was banned. It was available for a short time and then it disappeared.

Whose base is it on the moon? Is it the Grays or the lizards, which may also be known as Reptilians.

Linda:
Or anybody else?

Echo:
Hmn indeed. This be much as an, here refer, universal base, there do both that of the Reptilians and the Grays, at present here. Both the small Grays and the large Grays, and the Reptilians be present here.

Linda:
Could you comment on others who may be there as well and describe them please?

The Echo:
There be...somewhat difficult of description. Be those that appear of, approximate in thy understanding, 8-9 feet, distinctly straight in their structure. Oh...refer here, somewhat furried. Much as an, oh here refer, strong humanoid features, you understand.

Linda:
Are these the ones that disappear around people?

The Echo:
Indeed refer disappear?

Linda:
Well, the ones that...

(To Author) You used the term just now.

The Echo:
Ah the entity refer to that colloquially termed…Big…

Author:
Sasquatch.

The Echo:
…Foot…

Linda:
Sasquatch.

The Echo:
Sasquatch. Yeti.

Linda:
Are they the ones?

The Echo:
Indeed . Be similar. These refer Sasquatch, Yeti, these that…oh somewhat, here refer, stranded upon the planet from that of approximate time, in thy time understanding, approximate uh 3,000 years prior to beginning of present time usage.

Author:
Are you saying that the Sasquatch on Earth have been stranded here for 3,000 years before our history began?

The Echo:
Indeed.

Author:
I did not quite understand…and in answer to Linda's question, are they the same entities on the moon, these 8-9 foot tall, furried creatures, or are they similar?

The Echo:
They be similar.

Author:
OK. Nothing to do with each other.

The Echo:
Indeed not.

Linda:
I am going to ask another question. The Yeti, are they the ones that were stranded 3,000 years ago or is this another group?

The Echo:
Indeed. We speak of all.

Author:
You once called the Sasquatch the other society. Could you explain what that means?

The Echo:
Indeed so. Sasquatch are the other society, you understand. These entities exist within that of the planet Earth, in most areas of the planet Earth, and these entities maintain a near, near invisibility due to their need for, that refer, privacy, understand. The entities have not of wish…uh…to associate with that of the white-skinned. They have not of any need or desire to associate with that of the, refer, the human entity that be desecrating their homelands. They merely as they come upon those of the, refer, human race, they merely frighten them away in order that they be no longer within their presence.

Author:
Would it be possible for human beings and Sasquatch to communicate, if each group wanted to?

(Tape ends and is turned over. Some words lost)

Author:
Are you saying then the Sasquatch do not have spoken language?

The Echo:
Indeed not.

Author:
Now this may be a judgment, but so we understand. Their society…where does it stand? How advanced is their society compared to human society? In such things as taking care of their own species or love or ….

The Echo:
Indeed, in that of the taking care of their own species, they be far exceeding that of the human animal. Eh, love be of extreme format, loyalty each to the other be of extreme format. The entities do not speak in language such as thee, however, they do, indeed, emit sounds that be understood each by the other for particular means. It be that their language do not contain that which…oh, the human proudly state is syntax.

Linda:
You said that these apes, these people…the entities on the other side of the moon. They are not the ones that we see on our planet now? Were they originally on the moon? Is this a different race?

The Echo:
Hhmm indeed. You understand. Within, that refer, thy universe, beyond that of which thee refer universe, thy universe is only one small gathering of marbles in a massive area of others. They be an large number of, oh here refer, hmm, hmmn, intelligent beings that exist in many other reaches of the, oh here refer, universe for lack of a larger term, you understand. And these entities have indeed developed, a number of these groups have developed a means of travel within the firmament of space and these be of many different types of development. For there be those that exist upon two legs; there be those than exist upon four legs; there be those that do not use legs, you understand. There be all manner of creatures that have developed into intelligence through their own means and manners, and be

highly difficult to explain to thee the characteristics, the shapes, or the ideas of these entities due to their specializations, you understand.

Linda:
The fiction that we have heard, these tall men attempting to control, I don't know how many years ago...with David...

The Echo:
Goliath, in, that refer, Bible?

Linda:
Yes. Where they were fighting this 8-9-foot-tall man? This was supposedly fiction.

The Echo:
Hmn, indeed. That of the form, refer Goliath, merely be of an abberation of growth within its own culture and it be of approximate 8 feet in physical structure. That of the, here refer, giant...ohhmm...refer fables of the tribes of giants be brought down through the viewing of those that step upon the planet, eh from elsewhere and remain only very short duration.

Linda:
Fiction with a degree of truth.

The Echo: Indeed so.

Author:
(To Linda)
Most ideas that people have had about other kinds of beings, have been based on truth. They did not just make it all up. The ideas may be distorted, but they are based on truth.

The Echo:
Indeed so.

Author:

Another question. This is about something I heard on a late-night radio program. There is a theory that petroleum, or oil, that we find in the Earth, is not from animal or plant fossils. There is a theory that it is a self-generating substance. Could you comment?

The Echo:
Hmmm indeed. We will state to thee that, refer, oil, uh that refer in thy terms, crude oil, is indeed not generated by the extinction of animals or the dissolution of the bodies of animals, you understand. This is an substance that is produced by that of the planet Earth…eh through the, here refer, hmm, hmm eh filtration process of waters…eh from the surfaces through the rocks, the porousnesses of the planet, bringing with it that of the oils of plants, the oils that exist in grasses, you understand. And this is then leached through that of the, refer, filtration system of the planet and deposited in that of the, oh, oh refer, shearings of the Earth, the caverns that then become storage holders, you understand.

Author:
So oil does not come from dinosaurs. There is some plant substance in what we call crude oil?

The Echo:
Indeed so.

Author:
So theoretically, the planet need never run out of oil?

The Echo:
Hmm indeed. Unless that of the oil is used at a rate exceeding its ability to produce. You understand, an entity may never run out of drinking water if it is next to a pond, unless all the population drinks from the same pond.

Linda:
Are you saying there are other areas oil could be got?

The Echo:
Indeed. That of the investigations of those interested in the use of oil have located most of the deposits.

Linda:
Are you saying 75 per cent?

The Echo:
We would not draw a close line as the oils be, as it were, regenerating.

Linda:
So we are actually running out of oil?

The Echo:
Indeed so. The, here refer, madness of the entities upon the planet demand more and more oil. Indeed that of the availability will decrease. Do the entities stop using oil for a period of approximate 200 years, the oil deposits will return to their original state.

Linda:
Oh, boy...200 years.

(Listeners comment about the long duration of the wait.)

The Echo:
Indeed, this will create a creaking wagon.

(Laugher)

Linda:
Echo, Is there anything that you feel would be helpful for Patrick in the book that he is doing?

The Echo:
Indeed, that the entity merely continue with confidence, understand. The understanding that its skill, that its writings, will be received and recompense is available to the entity.

Author:
There is one more area. Last time I asked you a question. I said can people in the physical realm, in the physical body help you, The Echo, and the tape ran out so I did not get the answer. What if the people in this room were to send you thoughts of love and peace? Could you sense that and how would it help you?

The Echo:
Indeed. We would state to thee, in thy colloquial terms, all contributions gratefully accepted.

(Laughter)

The Echo:
Love be, indeed, be of highest receipt by we.

Author:
Would it take just conscious thought to say we are now sending The Echo love?

The Echo:
Indeed so. It be sufficient. You understand that of the reason of our approach is for our personal growth and development. Each query, each time an entity request information, uh, this also add to our growth possibilities, you understand. To assist others is a great means of we developing and growing within the spiritual realm, for we are not, here refer, those that know everything. We are also in learning format, you understand. Do accept love offered by others from the physical realm is indeed an high honour for we and we accept gratefully, you understand.

(Linda asks question about Cliff's purpose and her purpose in life being to assist each other)

The Echo:
Indeed it be correct. The form of the one Clifford have a purpose to assist thee through thy growth and development in life. Thee have a purpose in thy life to assist the form Clifford in

his growth and development through life. And we of The Echo have the purpose to assist as many as is possible in their growth throughout life.

Linda:
Thank you.

Author:
One other point. The last time I asked what it is like where you are your answers were matter-of-fact. You did not say it is a joyful place of love and peace.

The Echo:
Indeed so this be true, you understand. Remove from thy mind the image of 200-300,000 spirits...eh standing in a cluster waiting to answer a query, you understand. For it is not in this manner. Each and every entity in spirit is much as, oh here in thy understanding, much as a sparkle of light and there be little communication between each. However, as we have requested, refer, the entity Golude to behave as our spokesperson for the form of the one Clifford, as there be query offered to spirit, then that of the availability of answer is, here refer, somewhat selected from a sparkle of light. To explain the workings in this realm in the understandings of thy physical realm is a near-impossibility. And if thee hear an entity speaking to thee and stating that it is this way or it is that way, you understand, it is the physical entity speaking.

Author:
OK. I just thought that maybe we would get a description of Heaven. (Laughing)

I have read things...maybe it was spirit guides who told people that they are in a joyful place, there are no limitations, they can bilocate.

The Echo:
Indeed so. This be true. We do not however, oh as it were, walk along pathways in flowered gardens, you understand.

Author:
Could you not, if you wanted to? With thought projections could you not create that environment for yourselves?

The Echo:
Indeed so. We ask thee, though, to what purpose?

Author:
Ah...is a purpose of life not to experience the joy of life itself. Is a positive life not better than a negative life?

The Echo:
Indeed, We see not of, that refer, negative life.

Author:
That is the most that I have from you. You are not saying that you are in a blissful state, but you are saying that you are free of limitations or problems or negativity.

The Echo:
Indeed so.

Author:
So we do have something to look forward to, when we join you in the spirit realm?

The Echo:
Indeed so. You understand, to place that of thy human language words upon that of sensations that occur in the, refer, spirit realm is a near impossibly. We state to thee that indeed bilocation be not of difficulty. To be viewed, viewing of the lives, the existences of others in the physical realm oftimes is, refer, simple mater, other times not quite so simple matter. For oftimes, as we have prior stated, it be as viewing a signpost in a foggy dark night, you understand.

Author:
Yes.

Linda:
Echo, I have a question. Would you mind changing Cliff's position?

The Echo:
Uh…is that your question?

(Laughter)

Linda:
Part of it.

Author:
(To Linda)

You do not want to waste your questions… it is like with a genie rubbing the lamp.

Linda:
People often see ghosts. And these people (ghosts) are completely unaware of anybody else in our physical. The church has said these…people who are not in hell but…

The Echo:
Hhmm. Indeed That which they have termed purgatory.

Linda:
Yes.

The Echo:
Understand, the term purgatory has been coined in order to control those yet within the physical realm. To state to they, "You behave and do as we say or you will be condemned to an eternity of hell, or an eternity of floating about aimlessly, understand. This be an, here refer, man-made concept.

Linda:

OK. The way you have described it. It did not make any sense that... This is the first level after crossing over, and you are on higher levels, so you are not involved in that. And I think this first level is where (words unclear) people...

The Echo:
Of occasion, also there be that of a resonance of an action, of an activity, of which the entity have entered into in its physical existence and those resonances, as it were, be imprinted in the universal fabric and those entities that be of sensitivity can then view these activities and these persons, and these be termed ghosts.

Author:
It is interesting that you said that spirits are like sparkles of light. I have mentioned before that many evenings I can walk into a darkened room and see specks of light or sparkles of light, little slivers of light, all around.

The Echo:
Indeed, thee be surrounded.

(Asides)

Linda:
They are here right now.

Author:
I have not yet developed to the point of seeing them in the daylight.

The Echo:
We would allow the entity Clifford, at this point, to withdraw.

Linda:
Would you mind putting Cliff back in the position he was in when he started, please?

The Echo:

Indeed.

Linda:
We thank you for this session Echo.

The Echo:
And we The Echo thank thee of the opportunity of approach.

Therefore we say to thee, "Go in peace. Go in love and understandings."

We release the form.

(Author's Note: In November, 2006, the Echo said during a session that the decision to make information available to the public by the Grays had been delayed because of war on Earth.)

Chapter 6
"The Star People" by Brad Steiger

1983

Director:
May we proceed with questions?

The Echo:
Indeed. We will assist to the utmost of our ability.

Director:
>Echo, this evening we would like to discuss a book called "The Star People" by Brad Steiger. We are wondering if you would tell us how all this began, people on Earth and so on. "Star People" suggests that Extra-Terrestrials started a farm colony on this planet. Would you please start from there and explain?

The Echo:
>Indeed. Understand here. Far beyond that refer "Atlantean time", in that which be lost in antiquity, there be that of the searching of areas that may be used in an experimental fashion. Here, there be scoutings from that refer "Sirius" and that refer "Arcturus". And these entities find their friendly atmosphere on a planet, Earth, and here there be a descent of those travellers.in effect, there be here settlers. These individuals be of approximate eight feet, be golden skin-tones and be mainly those refer "prisoners" in your understanding. In effect here then, that of the planet Earth become a penal

colony, and there be constant observation of this colony by those refer "Intergalactic Travellers".

That of these entity break into portions... correction here...group that be in various locations about that of the planet. Those in region of that present refer "Russia" maintain height and physical structure through that of the here refer "millennia". Those in that area refer.....presently "Africa", tend here to dwarf somewhat throughout the many years. These entity then maintain that of a mean height of approximate five feet, seven or eight inches.

There be here an gradual dispersment of the entities throughout that of the land mass areas. Those then of the, reference, Arabic regions be of approximate five feet, seven or eight inches in height. These then encounter those entity from the north and west and these be observed as Giants in the land. That of the Giants in the land also be of a lighter skin colouring and of higher technological retentions. These entity then mate with the female of the smaller races and this bring about gradual loss of height among the peoples. Be then the blendings of the peoples.

There be here that of the watching of this development that cause visitors from, that refer, "Space" to land here and be greeted as the fathers of the "Golden Ones". These entity then be treated as "Gods" because they appear from the skies and disappear into the skies. In present, there be here that refer descendants of the "Star People."

That refer here "Star People" be of originally same stock as that of others in resonance of planet Earth. Therefore, here, do not assume that descendancy from that refer "Star People" create an effect speciality about one, as this is untrue.

Director:

That explains why I felt so vehement about that book. I didn't want to .....

The Echo:

Indeed so.

Director:

OK. Echo, you said that we could best understand the Star People coming to planet Earth as somewhat... as a penal colony. Could you expand on this please?

The Echo:
Indeed. As previous stated, there be that of the searchings for an area, planet, of which there may be experimentation performed. Here, that of those sent to that of planet Earth, be those that be especially and socially outcast among those of, reference, Space Persons. It be then that there be observation of these entities. Firstly, to observe their actions and reactions in a new unknown environment.
Secondly, observation to ensure these entities remain on planet Earth.

Director:

Why were they outcast in the first place ?

The Echo:

Indeed.

Understand, that of reference here, "The Council of Peers". It be that these entity act in negative and/or anti-social manner and be then, in effect here, evicted, banned of their home-land.

Director:

Could you tell us a little bit more about the civilization of Arcturus ?

The Echo:
Indeed. There be, here, high degree of technology. There be, here, that of the understanding of the electrostatic, electromagnetic constructions of the universe. There be here little of the needs of, that refer, fuel consumptions. There be, here, that of the use the reference "Anti-Gravity Nodes". That of the peacekeeping be in a manner of scanning of the planet and that of any negativity be shown on monitoring devices. Those then in negative mode be removed in order that peace be maintained.

Director:
How were they able to scan the planet? Was there something in peoples' brains? Was something implanted?

The Echo:

Indeed not. There be that of a scanning of the energy force, energy fields about each and every entity. This be, in effect, that of an aura scanner. Negativity then be clearly defined.

Director:
So did this wrongness in the aura carry down through the ages?

The Echo:
Indeed. Into that of, reference here, planet Earth. Understand. That of the physical beings in that of the planet Earth find extreme simplicity in involvement of negative thought and somewhat difficulty in that of involvement of positive thought.

Director:

In what time frame did the first colonizations occur?

The Echo:

Indeed. This be in query that of planet Earth ?

Director:

That's correct.

The Echo:

Indeed. That of approximate here of 100 millions of years in time, in time as you know it. There be here that of a following implantation, that of approximate 100,000 of years prior that of the beginnings of present calendar usage.

Director:

What happened to those who were here before?

The Echo:
Indeed. In that of the evolvement of the several, indeed many, of civilization structures, the entities have, through greed and avarice...created destructions of their civilizations. Each entity surviving than revert to animalistic existences. Then there be periods of re-evolvement that be necessary prior the forming of the next social structure.

Director:

Who or what was on the planet before these colonies of Star People came here?

The Echo:

Indeed. Not else.

Director:

In other words, they created life structure on the planet ?

The Echo:

Indeed so. That of reference "Human".

Director:

Were there animals and trees and things right there?

The Echo:

Indeed so.

Director:

Did they alter geographical landforms and bring about the island of Atlantis, or anything like that?

The Echo:

Indeed. Understand: That refer Atlantis be one of the many civilization risings and fallings. Also here understand: That refer Atlantis, there be of encompassment of the planet Earth and in that of the final days, the final years of this civilization, it be merely that of the area of the planet refer Atlantic Ocean of present.

Director:
Who then, is Satan? I mean, that name has come down through the ages.

The Echo:
Indeed. Understand here, in that of the de-evolvement of man, it become highly involved with its environment. That it thus co-exist within rules and regulations set by the environment.
The entities then place upon certain aspects of their existence that of a personification. It be here, in that of

the superstitious aspects of these entities., that there then be a name.."Satan ... evil doer, or, indeed, the unbeliever.

This be presented much as in your existence, that refer "bogyman". This be a fictional character, that of the personification of evil.

Director:

There is something in the Bible about fallen Angels or Watchers, apparently, these were men who had ..let me see...they were supposed to be the sons of God that were fallen and they mated with the daughters of men, who were here on Earth, and they became a very strong race of people. They descended from these people. Now they were known as Fallen Angels or watchers. How did that...

The Echo:

Understand here: As previous stated, these entity come from the North, mate with those of the smaller beings from the South. There be this event create necessity of those in observation of the planet to be in approach. These entity land and be observed as Gods and those from the North be then assumed to be the sons of the Gods. Those of the North retain their technological understandings and be in awareness of the approach of those from that refer "Outer Space".

Director:

I see. OK. You mentioned in an earlier session, that Adam and Eve were symbology of how ....

The Echo:

Indeed so.

Director:

They were symbolical of having been evicted from the Garden of Eden. In other words, the positive society of...

The Echo:

Indeed so.

Director:

I see. So it's allegorical of the seeding of the planet, is that correct?

The Echo:
Indeed so. Understand: it be that of the informations being carried through, that refer, "millennia" and this be naturally twisted, distorted, misrepresented, misunderstood.
Understand: That of the writings of which you speak here in relation Bible, be written by persons in the time-frame of existence when there be no knowledge of the flying individuals. There be no knowledge of man other than which exist within their immediate view. Therefore writings will be frustrated.

Director:
How then did woman come to be the personification of the cause of all the evil things that happened to man?

The Echo:

Alas, it be an man's world.

Director:

What happened in the area of the Dead Sea? What caused the Dead Sea to become dead?

The Echo:

Indeed. That of the shrinking of the core of the planet. That of the dropping of the land mass to that of low levels and that of the atomic explosions that be used in the manner of the attempt of eradication of those of negative thought.

Director:

So Sodom and Gomorrah were the real thing?

The Echo:

Indeed. The real thing.

Director:

Could you please tell us about it?

The Echo:

Indeed. There be that of the moral decay of the entities in physical existence of this area. These entity be approached from above. Be advised that of the altering of ways and this advisement be ignored. Therefore, a decision be reached to allow that of the removal of this stain from the experiment.

Director:

What were the people of Sodom and Gomorrah doing that was so horrendous?

The Echo:

Indeed. In the eyes of the watchers, there be that of total mistreatment of the fellow man on a scale, never since, nor before, repeated. The be that of the physical mutilation in order of the enjoyment of the mutilators, that of high degree of sexual deviances et cetera, et cetera.

Director:

So the watchers made the decision?

The Echo:

Indeed so.

Director:

Are those we are calling the Watchers, aware of spirituality like we are, understanding Karma, Reincarnation and that type of thing?

The Echo:

Indeed so. Understand, however: This be in a manner of experimentation of psychological and physical aspects of these entity. That of observed failure of the experiment in one area, then it be desire of the removing of this block of the experiment.

Director:

So we could view it as a laboratory situation?

The Echo:

Indeed so.

Director:

One cage of rats goes bad, you toss it out. Right? Was it really an atomic blast?

The Echo:

Indeed so.

Director:

What we know as a nuclear device?

The Echo:

Indeed. That of, reference here, of approximate 100 megatons blast.

Director:

Why would they use that when they have other means?

The Echo:

Indeed. Understand: In that of experimentation here, many informations may also be derived beyond that of the reference "blast".

Director:

So the blast itself was an experiment ?

The Echo:

Indeed so.

Director:

OK. I guess that makes some kind of sense. Along with that legend, that we have passed down via the Bible, I guess it is pretty accurate, then. The story of Sodom and Gomorrah is reasonably accurate in the Bible then?

The Echo:

Indeed so. Merely misrepresented.

Director:
> There was also the story of Lot's wife looking back just as the city was exploded. She was reportedly turned into a pillar of salt. What is that all about?

The Echo:

Indeed. This be merely that of a manner of speaking, as in that of a pillar of salt be reasonably useless. That of Lot's wife, in looking back was instantly blinded and be, in effect, useless.

Director:

I have heard of studies that were done on that and scholars had figured it was an atomic blast in Sodom and Gomorrah, because the description of someone that close to the blast would be actually white for a period of time, the person would be chapped so very quickly.

The Echo:

Indeed so.

Director:

Echo, there are similar large deserts in Arizona and Nevada. What is the cause of that?

The Echo:

Indeed. Understand here: This be, that refer, sea bottoms here.

Director:

Were the seeders themselves seeded from other places in the Galaxy or Universe. What was their origin?

The Echo:

Indeed. There be that of a seeder's appearing in that of a land refer Minault, and this indeed be to that of implant of the planet Earth. These be woods that be non-resonant to that of other woods of the planet Earth.

Director: Oh, OK. You misunderstood my question. I said it incorrectly. What I meant was the seeders of the planet, the Watchers, those who put human forms on Earth.

The Echo:

Indeed. We speak of a plant in the growing.

Director:

Right, sorry about that. Those who established the penal colony, what shall we call them? So shall we call them the Watchers for a reference?

The Echo:

Indeed. Here refer "Arcturians".

Director:

"Arcturians". OK. Where did the Arcturians actually come from?

The Echo:

Indeed. Arcturia.

Director:

Well. they must have come from another planet. Did they spring up out of the middle of Arcturius?

Like, were they not a colonization from somewhere else, originally ?

The Echo:

Indeed. Understand here: That of the delving here further require that of the deepening of the trance state, as this be lost in antiquity.

Director:

This point we will pause and I will turn the tape over. Echo, at this time can you tell me what level the form of Cliff is at, please ?

The Echo:

Indeed. The form of the one Clifford, trance state J, level 8542 maintaining.

Director:

Thank you.

You mentioned also that Jesus was an implant. Did the watchers, the Arcturians, impregnate a female of this Earth ?

The Echo:

Indeed. Understand: There be that of the presentation here of the female, selected, in order that there may be one that may indeed be nurtured and grown.

Director:

To help remove negativity from the world ?

The Echo:

Indeed so.

Director:

This child, this Jesus... I'm having a little difficulty there. I'm sorry,..this child Jesus, the soul, that was born to this baby... How did the Arcturians choose a soul so understanding, so already understanding, that they could nurture it no further ?

The Echo:

Indeed. Here do not assume that of the choosing here of the soul. It be merely that of impregnation and careful nursing.

Director:

Then how was it that his coming had been predicted for so long?

The Echo:

Indeed. Understand: That of the prediction be maintained of hundreds of years. It be that of the cry of a needing people. Here it be merely that of designed fulfillment of those prophesies.

Director:

Designed fulfilling ?

The Echo: Indeed. so.

Director: Is that where the Essenes came in ?

The Echo: Indeed so.

Director: Were they in contact with the Extra-Terrestrials?

The Echo: Indeed.

Director:

Directly?

The Echo:

Indeed so. Understand: There be that here of somewhat of an conspiracy.

Director:

There seems to be a lot of controversy, shall we say, surrounding the conception of the one chosen, being immaculate....

The Echo:

Indeed so.

Director:

What is your interpretation of that?

The Echo:

Indeed. Firstly here: There be a secretive, although not that refer immaculate. Understand: Those in involvement here have not spoken all. they have partaken of.

Director:

I am still a little bit unclear about the situation. Joseph, father of Jesus, was he directly from Arcturus ?

The Echo:

Indeed not.

Director:

Would you then explain in more detail how this happened?

The Echo:

Indeed: That of the form Joseph be that in effect stepfather, as the entity in it's empathy do assist that of the female form, as the female form, in attaining state of pregnancy, be in danger of the stoning of it's physical body. That of a male entity then offer assistance in the format mate.

Director:

You say she was to be stoned because of Herod's decree, or some other reason ?

The Echo:

Indeed. Merely here because of that of the pregnancy foretold of the wicked woman.

Director:

Oh yes! Women were stoned for such things before they were officially married. OK. Let's hit it point blank: How did she actually conceive the child ?

The Echo:

Indeed. That of the encounter of that here refer "Extra-Terrestrial".

Director:

Was this done by...

The Echo:

Design. Indeed so.

Director:

A person, an Extra-Terrestrial then would have the positive vibrations about him that would create a chance of having a child of positive vibrations. Is that what you are saying ?

The Echo:

Indeed so.

Director:

But in essence, this was another experiment ?

The Echo:

Indeed so. And we may add here; Be here somewhat of a failure, as the understanding have be little developed in the animal man.

Director:

It was a good idea at the time, but in the long run, there is still a lot to be learned?

The Echo:

Indeed so.

Director: Echo, you mentioned that the Christos Spirit consciousness descended on Jesus, when he was baptized. Can you tell me how that was arranged?

The Echo:

Indeed. Understand here: In that of the dealing of spirituality, that of the dealing of the Extra-Terrestrials, there be here depths of understanding that in your knowings be of high degree difficulty of your understanding.

Director:

You mentioned earlier that there was a second seeding or implantation. Could you describe the events surrounding this?

The Echo:

Indeed. There be here that of the animal man return another time to that of animalistic nature and revert to that of hunting, killing, living with bare necessities. There then be that of further implant and there be here, once more, that of reference "eight feet tall entity" upon the face of the Earth. These entity then be in blending with that of present man and the resultant figures be in existence today.

Director:

I have another question about Extra-Terrestrial and Christos consciousness: Do these Extra-Terrestrial all have .... are they all. masters..! mean masters like Jesus, all in understanding of the universe?

The Echo:

Indeed. Understand: We do not recognize that of the term Masters. However, there indeed be a high degree of the development of understanding.

The form of the one Clifford gaining of rigidity.

Director:

How much longer would you suggest this session last?

The Echo:

Indeed. Here that of approximate three minutes in time, in time as you know. We must then release the form.

Director:

I have another question. You have been describing Extra-Terrestrial about eight feet tall, golden skin. Now there have been encounters of Extra-Terrestrials who have very large eyes and their skin is a white colour. Some are short and some are tall. Who are these people?

The Echo:

Indeed. Be not in the understanding that there be only one race.

Director:

Most people though, have not encountered these tall golden skinned people. We have heard about them, from thousands of years ago, but generally they have not been encountered in present day. Can you explain why?

The Echo:

Indeed. The entity here believe the experien.. correction, the experiment be abandoned ?

Director:

I don't know.

The Echo:

Understand: We wish to find the entity be in thinking mode.

Director:

I guess not... no, I don't think the experiment has been abandoned. It may well have been expanded.

The Echo:

Indeed so.

Director:

Is it starting to include other Extra-Terrestrials from other parts of the universe?

The Echo:

Indeed. There be a preparation for that of the encounter of other forms of existence.

Director:

I guess we will have to let that one hang. Is there anything you would like to say, Echo, before closing?

The Echo:

Indeed. Understand: that of the farm colony be millenia in, that refer, past. Understand: That of the present existence of planet Earth be an fine place to exist and you have the opportunity of more improvement here. Therefore, carry on in your development of the understandings, that you may one day assist others more fully in their understandings.

Director:

Thank you for this session.

The Echo:

Indeed. We of The Echo thank you for the opportunity of approach.

    Therefore we say to you,

                Go in Peace.
      Go In Love and Understandings.

Chapter 7
Extra-Terrestrials, Space Aliens

> ECHO SESSION
> MONDAY, JUNE, 15,1998
> 14 PERSONS PRESENT

Director:

Is all well with the form?

The Echo:

That of the form of the one Clifford, trance state H, level 943 broadening, naturally.

Director:
We would like this, all these questions to be on Extra-Terrestrials and aliens. Is there anything you would like to say before we start?

The Echo:

Indeed: We are.

Director:

We are what?

The Echo:

That refer extra-terrestrial or alien.

Director:

(laughing)

OK, tell us a little bit about that, then.

The Echo:

Indeed: Those that be in that refer Spirit realm, may indeed move freely in comparison to that here refer Earth bound entities. Therefore they may be then termed extra-terrestrial.

Director:

OK, but those are not the kind of questions we are going to ask you about, though. We would like to ask questions on what we would normally consider Extra-Terrestrials.
So is there anything you would like to add to that before we ask those questions?

The Echo:

Indeed: Merely here the understanding that thee need not be that here refer conceited in the thoughts that thee be the only creatures within the universe.

Director:
That's certainly how most of us feel, anyway.

It would have been about the fall of 1979, I had an out-of-body experience and I found myself in a spaceship and I saw these two people, they were working over some kind of machinery, and I was just watching and suddenly they became aware that I was there. They turned around and began to walk towards me. Now what I saw, was not exactly the way you see them in pictures. Like they seemed, in the pictures, they seemed much shorter. These seemed to be in white gowns, of course, they didn't have hair, and they did have those very large black eyes.
Now, was I imagining this, or, oh, then suddenly, when they became aware of me and started towards me, it frightened me and I slammed back into my body

The Echo:
Indeed, that refer Run and Hide Syndrome.

(Group Laughter)

Director:
Yes, Yes. Why is what I saw different from the books that talk about alien beings?

The Echo:
Indeed: Understand, in that of, here your terms, in most cases, those that be in the presentation of writings, be not in the viewing thereof. Understand, these entity be in the gathering of informations from others, and place upon paper an drawing format that which they assume the other have encountered. The other, then in the noticing of the drawings, indeed believe that this be an fair representation.
Within the instance of self, thee be not in the viewing of that here refer the wee green men.

Do understand, the entity be in the viewing of those that be in some degree form here refer, Mantis, and be of approximate six feet in general height patterns.

Director:
So the persons that I saw were six feet tall?

The Echo:
Indeed so.

Director:

And .... they saw me, even though I was out-of-body at that time?

The Echo:

Indeed so.

Director:

OK. I didn't feel they were negative, but it frightened me. Why were they approaching, what would they have done, if I had stayed?

The Echo:

The highest probability be to that here of salutations.

Director:

Very nice. So they would have been communicating telepathically?

The Echo:

Indeed so, and in that here refer, friendly.

Director:

Great! I know a person, who when she channels, she says it is an extra-terrestrial speaking through her. A person who has not passed over, just speaking through her. Does this happen to many people?

The Echo:

Indeed, of occasion, do the entity so allow. Indeed so.

Director:

M., do you have a question?

Echo, do you need to turn Cliff around to talk with M.?

The Echo:

Indeed. That refer M.? Location.

Director:

He's directly behind you.

The Echo:

Indeed. We will gain further control of the physical being as we progress.

Director:

OK, go ahead.

M.

Echo, these questions have something to do with the reading of the Kryon books #2.
Are you familiar with that, where they talk about the Others, outside of Earth? One question here would be, on the positive side, I had a dream where there was a spaceship and there were.... you had indicated before these people were here to help me in some way... but what I am interested about in some of the reading I've been going through, is.... there are some names, and I would like you to tell me if these Extra-Terrestrials are from one or more of these groups. That would be the Arcturians/Ashtar, or the Pleidians, which I am told are the seed group for humans here on Earth.

The Echo:

Indeed: That of the Pleidians, indeed so.

M. ....

Right. So they are the ones that are seen by us here on at least a couple of occasions, and they are close by us, watching us and in fact walk among us, because they have the same biology?

The Echo:

Indeed so. The forms of the one Clifford, the one Linda, encountered an here refer mated pair of Pleidians, of approximate 1985 within that city refer Guelph.

Director:

Oh! I remember that! We were in a restaurant!

M.........

The understanding is that these entities have to be very, very careful, not to show too much because they have...I guess my understanding is they are about 260,000 years ahead of us in terms of technological advancement. So they can only share what they know as is appropriate and must be very careful about disclosing too much.

The Echo:

Indeed so. Do understand, it be here akin to self, returning to that here in your terms, that refer caveman days, and asking for the time. Do understand.

Director:

Echo, there was a time, I guess that would have been about 1984, in Prince Edward county. I was outside, on the porch looking outside and I saw this light in the sky. It was night time. I saw this light in the sky. It was moving very quickly and I thought "It must be extra-terrestrial" and I heard this voice say Yes. It stopped, the light going out, and then further along it came on again and went zipping out of sight. Now, what I heard in my mind, was that imagination. Was what I saw, really nothing? What did I see that evening?

The Echo:
Indeed, that refer here in your terminology, an extra-terrestrial craft. Indeed so. Understand, merely in the viewing, there be contact. Understand, in the viewing, it be as though the entity turn, to an , in your understanding, radio dial station and send an frequency that be received and understood by that upon which thee view. In this manner, it then be enabled to enter to thee and reply.

Director:
It seems like, when we travelled a lot, that we would miss 20 minutes or an half-hour and it started to get a little irritating. We weren't physically uncomfortable, it just affected our time. Now why was this occurring?

The Echo:
Indeed, in your colloquial, it be an matter of "checking in". Understand, the entities, both, the form Clifford, the form Linda, be in that here refer implantation format of the region refer Vancouver Island and the entities be then repeatedly examined in order to insure all be well.

Director:
I always felt Extra-Terrestrials there. It also happened when we were travelling from Winnipeg to Fort Frances, quite frequently. So they are just checking up, then? We haven't experienced anything for about four or five years.

The Echo:
Indeed: Not in an matter of noticement.

QUESTION:
I feel I have had a great deal of exposure to ETs, is this correct?

The Echo:
Indeed the entity be aware.

QUESTION:
I seem to have lost contact over the last couple of years or so. What can I do in meditation or on the spiritual plane to re-connect that?

The Echo:
Indeed: Merely request that channels of communication be clear. Beyond that, the entity perhaps wait.

QUESTION:
I want to know about my Egyptian connection. Also, I lost an hour last week Monday and I wanted to know if I was just phasing out or what?

The Echo:

Firstly here do understand, that of the refer Egyptian culture, be viewed by those in existence of present, as an early format of that refer present day culture. Do understand this be untrue, as that in the understanding of the planet Earth to present, there have been approximate 200 civilizations rising and failing, and that of the cultures of the Egyptian, of the pyramids, of the statues, be indeed created prior that which be referred Egyptian culture of present. The pyramids be set in their positions in order of the creation of electronic beacons that create an beaconry to direct , here refer, entities, to the planet Earth.
Do understand: The symbols, the symbologies, be directly related to that refer the Pleidians.

QUESTION:
The things they made with gold and had that powerful energy coming through it, is this what you are referring to?

The Echo:
Indeed: Do understand, that refer the "Ark of the Covenant" be an communication device that be self-generating in energy and the technology be presented to the planet throughout that, here refer, Extra-Terrestrials.

Director:
So, it really did exist?

The Echo:

Indeed so.

Director:

Is it still here somewhere, or is it broken up? Is this the same as the portal where humans come into life and go out of life? Like in the time of Moses when this was carried about or held in temple and if a normal human even touched it, he would be electrocuted by the strength of the energies?

The Echo:

Indeed: Refer Portal to the spiritual and Portal to the Spiritual. The entity be deeply engrossed in its "Playing" and so lost an hour. The entity also, however, be in the refer : taken, as it were by that refer Grays and the entity be examined by the Greys. The entity will find there be an examination mark on its upper right buttock close to the base of the spine. Be not of danger, be not of difficulty.

QUESTION:
My next question I have here is about the Greys. My understanding is that they are called Zetta. Is that correct?

The Echo:
The term may be applied in a certain society. Of the society of present, term Greys.

QUESTION:
With respect to the Greys, it is that they are attracted to humans because they lack the emotions that humans have. There is currently channeling coming through from the Greys and as of about 1985, there have been shifts in the energy of the Earth and so humans are now becoming increasingly aware of their free choice and this is frightening the Greys and that basically they are lying to us. They are trying to intimidate us through fear, to allow them to study us because they are interested in our emotions; and understanding. Yet we need a human link to understand that we do have free choice, that if we demand, number one, that they ask our permission before we are examined and number two, that we can refuse to be examined and because of the laws of nature, they must obey this and so, if we understand this we can in fact permit examination or refuse it and they must obey. They are in fact learning the lesson of honouring others.

The Echo:
Indeed so. Understand, an entity that be approached by here refer "Greys", the entity may, in it's decision, refuse accompaniment. This then be an matter of decision of that refer be in your terms,

upon Spiritual level and an entity in refusal will then be not further encountered.

M.......
Is it true that the "Greys" are currently lying to us through human channels, saying that there is some sort of contract with our governments, etc., etc., because they are afraid actually of losing the contract by us choosing not to grant to them.

The Echo:
Indeed. Understand, there indeed be that refer contract. However, the contract be broken, and here refer violated. As the contract be that thee may here refer "Greys", may be examine individuals within the accepted will of the individual and without physical harm or fear to an individual. This have been violated numerous occasions. Therefore, that of contract be null and void.

M...
My understanding is they do this by playing on people's fear. People become fearful and then they become submissive or able to be manipulated in this way.

The Echo:
Indeed so. Understanding be the use of that refer strongest, comparative tool.

L.

When was the last time I allowed them to do this me? When did I refuse?

The Echo:
Indeed. An approximate three months.

L...
Oh! Only three months?

The Echo:

Indeed so.

L.

I have a question about crop circles. Are the crop circles being made by higher-elevated beings than the Greys, or are they interested in us to the highest form of good?

The Echo:

Indeed not. Do understand: These be an means of attempted communication with the planet. We would suspect that these entities be highly amused at the antics of the humans in the attempt of explanation of this format.
Do understand, an highly mathematical symbol, covering the length and breadth of an entire field may hardly be manifested by an man carrying an piece of string and an board. Do also understand, in the examination of this format, there be not found that refer footprints or damages to the croppings in approach or retreat of these circles. These be highly complex mathematical symbols to assist those an Earth to be aware of others within, the universe and if necessary or if willed to indeed find those others.

Director:
Do they use more percentage of their brains than we do?

The Echo:
Indeed. There be a number of here refer varying races. Each be of separate origin, however, on average here they be using approximately 20%.

Director:
So they are a lot more intelligent that we are?

The Echo:

Indeed not. They are not more intelligent. They are merely using more., comparative, of their brains format.

M....
With respect to that, one question that came up is about intelligence. That humans here think sometimes that someone may be 200,000 years advanced in terms of technology, but relative to humans, they could very well be at caveman level in terms of enlightenment. We should not assume just because these people have the technology to come here, that they are in fact enlightened.

The Echo:

Indeed so.

Director:

Is everybody becoming abducted, and if not, who is most threatened ?

The Echo:
Indeed. Understand, most often it be of random choice. Of occasion it be that of the selection of particular individuals that be aware of the presences and therefore must needs be in the minds of that here refer Extra-Terrestrials, must then needs be examined in order to determine how is that these entity be aware and others are not.

V..... I would like to know who it is that is making the crop circles.

The Echo:
It be that of the, here refer, Extra-Terrestrial entities, and these be creating, that refer, crop circles, through an energy format that be presented by that of an, refer, small craft, and it be presented in order that there be communication availabilities with those located an planet Earth, and that those of planet Earth, in the

deciphering of the mathematical formulas will be aware of the location of others within the universe.

V.

Which race is doing this?

The Echo:
Indeed. There be that of that here which be in your terms, generally referred "Mantis". Understand, the Mantis also maintain within their environment, an smaller being, that be approximately three feet in height and these entities be much as you may refer worker bees in your environment. These entity then man the small ships that come extreme close of the planet and often use the energy of their vehicles to create that refer crop circles. Understand. The crop circles be not imprinted in an progressive manner. These be imprinted instantaneously, as the design within the vehicle be transmitted to the face of the planet.

L......
The Mantis you spoke of in the last session. You said it had been visiting me occasionally for about 10 years?

The Echo: Indeed so.

V....

Can you tell me of specific times, so that I might be able to remember?

The Echo:

Indeed. There be here viewed an time of anger within the entity, the entity moving to its private quarters, closing its being within and entering into an state of sorrow within its being and an state of anger within its being. The entity lay upon its bed and the entity lose, at this point of time the conscious recalling of approximate three hours in time. This be of approximate six and one half years prior of present.

Director:

What occurred to her then? What did they do?

The Echo:

Indeed. Examination.

Director:

How did they examine her?

The Echo:

Indeed. Carefully. The entity be removed. Indeed so.

Director:

Did they place some kind of implanted device in her?

The Echo:
Indeed not. There be not the viewing of this in this body. Understand, the entity in primary encounter be in format of examination. Beyond this format, the entity will be acutely aware of association of that refer any Extra-Terrestrial energy form.

**** Part 3 ****

Appendix

Other original transcripts of sessions

8. A personal Echo session	170
9. The Echo interpret dreams	180
10. Meditation – Automatic Writing	193
11. The Echo's Code of Living and Other Statements	211
Linda Preston's essay "Science Fiction?"	216
Conclusion	218

Chapter 8   A personal session with The Echo

The following is an excerpt from a written transcript of a client's personal session with The Echo. All client sessions are confidential. Permission was obtained to publish this excerpt, keeping the identities of the client and spouse confidential. Questions reproduced here range from health to psychic experiences. Most answers relating to health are specific to an individual. While there may be wider application for some of the advice, matters of individual health are best addressed individually.

November, 2000
St. Catharines, Ontario

Present: Cliff Preston, channeling The Echo
          Linda Preston, directing the session
          A client and spouse.

Client:
In April 2000, I first noticed a swelling in the bottom joint of the big toe in my right foot. Can you tell me about this?

The Echo:
This be a slight degree of calcification... insufficient intake of calcium. If the entity strike the joint gently, it will experience a severe sharp pain, more severe then the degree of striking call for.

Client:
That is surprising because I have always drunk milk.

The Echo:
The milk of the cow is for bovine creatures. While it contains calcium, it be insufficient for the human animal. (Words unclear) ...supplements, tablets.

Client:
Sometimes I have a prickling sensation on the top of my feet and on my ankles. Can you tell me what this is?

The Echo:
This be the result of the thought patterns of the entity, withholding... stressful patterns, then translate stresses throughout the physical body. In this instance, translate to the feet, upper portions and occasionally to the ankles of the entity. This be due to the intensity of the thought patterns of this entity and its need to understand. When the entity do not understand, it stress its physical being through its thought patterns.

Client:
The odd time my heartbeat seems to increase without any physical activity. Can you comment on this?

The Echo:
There be not of difficulties. If the entity enter into palpitations, the highest probability is nervousness-related. B vitamins each in conjunction with the other will indeed assist thee well. Overall, in general a fine state of health. The entity however be in requirement of the assistance of iron within its bodily functions. This may be obtained through greens such as dandelions, Swiss chard, spinaches and such as, or through, that refer, supplemental ingestion of iron. Therefore irons, calciums be of highest order for the entity.

Entity find degree of slowness of its being in the approximate hours of 1 pm to 2 pm each day. This be alleviated through the use of the iron.

Meditation be of fine format should the entity so desire. Finest format be that of entering into theta levels of brain wave pattern. In thy understanding deep meditation. The entity may find in this state it enter into a sleeplike state and awaken at the predetermined time.

Fishes for ingestion... use liberal amounts of, that refer, lemon juice on the fishes as it be of high degree acidic within the body and lemons be of high degree alkalinity upon entering the body. This negate the acidity. Beyond this, that of the addition of the calcium and the iron and ensuring a reasonable balance diet be of fine format. Of occasion do it desire that of the flesh of the animals, we suggest that it use only that of the flesh of the bovine, not the swine.

Client:
Twice I worked for a company which went through the process of reducing the number of its employees. Why did this happen twice? (Company names mentioned.)

The Echo:
It be merely, in thy terms of understanding, the coincidental entrapment of self in, here refer, in a somewhat losing situation.

Client:
This was not a message that I was in the wrong career?

The Echo:
Indeed, not.

Client:
Why have I have had difficulty re-establishing myself?

The Echo:
The entity, here to an degree, having entered into a life-change pattern, this life-change pattern occur to some individuals upon the opening to Spirit. Acceptance of understanding of Spirit create an, here refer, non-attraction of thy being to other individuals. It be subtle and the other individuals do not understand why there be non-attraction. However, it oftimes be

engineered through Spirit attempting to lead thee or assist thee in a slightly different direction and perhaps this entity... it behoove the entity to enter into a format of its own making and be not in the employ of another.

Client:
(Laughing)
Was this my unattraction to them or their unattraction to me?

The Echo:
This be engineering format from Spirit. It be somewhat likened to the placing of a shield about thee in order that others be not in view of thee. Therefore, do thee apply for a position, while the entities will speak with thee, there be not that attraction that will draw thee to employment. Be somewhat similar to that of the request from Spirit that thee take charge of thy own existence, as it were, and be thy own master.

Client:
Why have I always enjoyed writing comedy?

The Echo:
That of the writing of comedy be an expression of thy understanding of thy fellows. Be an understanding of the ridiculousness of regimentation and of rules and regulations. Therefore, this be inherent within the entity. Thee by all means continue with this format. Do the entity concentrate upon this facet of its existence, success pattern be assured for the entity within a time span of approximately less than two years.

Client:
I would like to ask about some psychic experiences.
The first is a memory from my childhood of a mental picture of some persons seated at a table in a tent. This was a clear image that I still remember. I think I had my eyes closed as I was lying in bed. It might have been after dreaming, when I was just waking up.
In the visualization, I had the idea that it was the beginning of life. There was a line of individual adults moving to my left in

front of the figures at the table, who I sensed were giving the instructions or the guidelines for life. There were at least two figures, probably men, and possibly more figures, but I remember the two in the centre of the table the best. I sensed that most of the persons filing past would say "Thank you very much, but I know how to do it myself." Then they would leave. I seemed to be observing from in front and to my right of the table. I think I was a presence but did not have a body. I understood the proceedings telepathically. I felt upset and disappointed that no one that I saw was listening to the advice. I thought that this behavior was unadvisable. I wanted the seated figures to know that I would listen to the advice when I had the chance. I thought that I would certainly follow their advice.

I was also aware that some of the persons, who had said they knew how to do it, were coming back in, through another door, or tent flap. There seemed to be a sense of regret. A sense of sadness. A sense that if only they had listened to the advice. They filed past the table again and they seemed to say, "Sorry, I made a mistake."

I knew that because they would not listen, they had made serious mistakes. At least they came back and admitted that they had been wrong. Maybe they would listen now, but they had already been through difficulties. I did not have any idea of what would happen to them next.

The Echo:
Indeed. This indeed be that of an memory of thy, here refer, translation of the experience prior to birthing, you understand. It be that point in spirit, here refer, between physical existences at which the entity have entered into decision of the incarnational format. The entity then be in, oh, here refer, speaking to those, refer, spirit assistants, leaders, guides, that offer insight and understanding in order to assist the entity with its life decision prior to reincarnation. The entity carry this remembrance to its physicalness, and translate such as the lineup of individuals that be, here, not listening, then finding perhap shortness of physical existence and return for another… (*word unclear*)… type existence, you understand.

Client:
That is what I thought at the time. I had not thought of that scene in years.

Client:
In (year stated), I had the impression, or perhaps intuition, that (company named) was the wrong place for me and that I would never get ahead. I should not be working there. The wrong place and I would never advance.

The Echo:
In that instance, another of the marionettes. Marionettes do not grow, oh, large tree… marionettes stay the way they be…

Linda:
Echo would you mind changing Cliff's position again?

(Cliff's body stiffly assumes a different sitting position. There are some comments back and forth.)

The Echo:
…gain understandings.

Linda:
Well you did how many thousands of years ago? When you could do that.

The Echo:
Indeed within thy understanding, that be thousands of years. Expect we to be stiff.

(Laughter).

Client:
They are also clairvoyant. One of my written questions is that could The Echo tell us a joke that would make us laugh. They just did.

The Echo:
Indeed so.

Client:
You have a dry sense of humor.

Client.
I don't think that I allowed myself to think that I have a psychic power because I viewed that as something far away, or removed, from daily, modern life. It might also have seemed presumptuous that Spirit would contact me directly. But still I wondered.

A couple of years ago some incidents happened.
The first was in September, 1998. It was like a dream because I was lying down resting during the day, but I was not asleep. I was aware that I was lying down for a few minutes and that I did not want to fall asleep, but it must have been something like sleep. In a dream when I am communicating telepathically there is no physical body beside me. I am aware of another presence, but there is no body there. There are no spoken words. I am communicating instantaneously by exchanging ideas. There is no voice.
I was asking this other spirit, or this other entity, how can you see angels? We were looking at a shadow moving on a wall. The spirit said, "There are angels here now." I was quite impressed. I asked, "Well, how can you tell" because it seemed to be only a dark shadow. Just at that moment the angel appeared clear in the dark shadow. I heard a voice in my left ear, like a radio channel opening up, and definitely that was a voice, because before it had been telepathy, it had not been a voice. The voice said: "Hello (client's name). Now that (we or they) trust you to let you see (either us or them) and I did not get the rest of the message.
I had overwhelming feelings of love…of being accepted…of being included, recognized, validated, as if, all my life, if I were looking for something, this was it. I felt fulfilled and part of a whole.

The Echo:

Indeed. Understand the message be that since they, here refer, assistants, spirit guides, feel enough trust within thee and understand the love that be within thee...they do allow thee to view that, here refer, angel. This then be bestowed upon thee at the point of the opening of thy psyche and the connection to the, here refer, Spirit realm and or to that of the realm of God. Thee be offered the hand of assistance from Spirit to fully enhance thy existence in whichever manner thee do so desire. As the love, the understanding emanating from thee be recognized.

Linda:
Is this the spirit helping him with impressions that he has...

The Echo:
They will assist in the enhancement that of the clairvoyance, that of the clairaudience, that of the empathetic talents.

Linda:
Is this one also giving him impressions.

The Echo:
Will assist in all areas of existence.

Client:
In the same month, September, 1998, I was reading a book by James van Praagh, the medium. Then I thought I would try automatic writing because I had known about it for a long time, and I wanted to see whether I could receive a direct communication from Spirit. I sat at a desk by the window in the den. I was doodling and trying to let a spirit move the pen. Nothing happened for about 10 minutes, but then the window beside me started to rattle, just two feet away. I later learned from a news report on the radio that there had been a minor earthquake at that moment. Here I was trying to receive a communication from spirit and the window beside me rattled. It took my attention immediately. It was fun to think about. I was amused and pleased by it. I told (spouse named). I told one or two other persons about this. Was that a co-incidence? Or something special.

The Echo:
It be a demonstration to thee that thy power, thy strength, thy will, go far beyond that of the, here refer, mere phenomenon of automatic writing. You understand that it be that perhap term, prod to understand further.

Client:
Have I known any of the members of your group before?

The Echo:
Indeed so. In prior associations. Friendship format, in passing format and, of occasion, within personal format.

Spouse:
What can I do to help him develop his psychic gifts?

The Echo:
Firstly, support, and love be primary. Acceptance of the entity in its thought patterns. And fourthly, the order to him to do it.

(Laughter.)

The Echo:
That of the form Clifford. We waited patiently for 40 years before it would admit there be other than the physical.

Client:
Would spirits not know better how to communicate with us?

The Echo:
In your society, do an entity suddenly appear before thee, there may be response of fright or religious fervor. Therefore, an entity in spirit must ensure that an entity must be ready, in its own understanding, prior to contact.

(Session nears end.)

The Echo:
(*In response to unspecified question(s), passage possibly incomplete*)

It is to our benefit to assist, as this be a portion of our growth patterns. To further to that of the, here refer, the Source, or that refer, God, therefore, in assisting thee we assist we. In relation to the understanding of the human animal. We doubt this be possible as there be free choice and we may offer our objective wisdom, yet it remain to someone in the physical to accept or reject. Therefore, we do not maintain judgments.

Chapter 9   The Echo interpret dreams

The following are excerpts from written transcripts of a client's personal sessions about dream interpretation with The Echo as dated. All client sessions are confidential. Permission was obtained to publish these excerpts, keeping the identities of the client and spouse confidential.

St. Catharines, Ontario

Present: Cliff Preston, channeling The Echo
           Linda Preston, directing the session
           A client and spouse.

October 27, 2003

Client:
In my dream, I walked into a room and saw my deceased father sitting at table. He looked good and he looked happy. I asked what it is like on the other side. He did not seem to understand. I was concerned that there were a couple of bruises on his face. What does this mean?

The Echo:
Perhap a highly convoluted mind. We jest.

Subconsciousness of self bringing to thy realization that there do indeed be barriers between spiritual and physical. Communication between the two is at best mediocre. Bruisings merely indicate to thee that the entity is able yet to show thee its being in a physical manner. Bruisings presented so that entity realize that father, at this point, be both in physical and spiritual resonance. Entity has difficulty, degree, communicating with thee at present. Connotation may be that this communication opening wider, wider, wider, as thee progress further.

Client:
In another dream, I was in a camper with a few men. We had an idea that someone would be charged with murder if we were found. We were parked in a great place where no one would find us, so I never felt threatened. We had an idea that some men were in custody and were being questioned, but the dream faded.

The Echo:
Presentation to thee designed to quell thy fears of authority. Entity in growing from childhood has been indoctrinated in that, here refer, religious rules and regulations, and this be a message from subconscious portion of thee that, in reality, there be not of necessity for entity to hide from rules. The rules no longer be accepted by the entity, as the entity has learned to see far beyond they.

November 1-2, 2003

Client:
I was at a political banquet. I was speaking at a podium. There was a happy mood.

The Echo:
Out-of-body experience, in which entity indeed be presiding and presenting its ideas, opinions, thoughts to others. In another realm of reality that be possible realm of reality for this entity, do it so choose.

October, 2005

St. Catharines, Ontario

Present: Cliff Preston, channeling The Echo
          Linda Preston, directing the session
          A client.

Client:
I have some questions about dream interpretation because I think it would be interesting. I think that you, The Echo, do a very good job of dream interpretation.

(Linda laughing.)

I would not come to anybody who wasn't the best.

(Joint laughter)

I also never flatter anybody. You know that.

The Echo:
We are not flattered.

Client:
No, I don't think you would be flattered. I think you take everything objectively and literally.

OK. Starting with a recent dream.

Saturday, September 24/05   Approximately 7:30 am.

    Linda Preston was sitting on a straight chair with her back to the door way. Cliff Preston standing on her left side which was my right as I viewed the scene. We were about to do something, perhaps channeling.
    Linda said that she felt a presence. She suggested that we open the door and let the presence enter. Her hair started blowing gently forward as a presence developed. There was an idea that we would open the door, but the door opened on its own and

Cliff stepped forward out of the way. I thought that this was wonderful because I thought that an invisible presence had joined us.

I could see around the door and out into the hall. There was no physical being there. Then as I was viewing the hall, the door closed on its own.

I thought that this was a sign. I was not sure whether this was an ordinary dream or a lucid dream, but I had the belief that this was an important incident. I believed that it was a clear sign in a dream because it does not happen in waking life. A sign which I was aware of and would remember. My consciousness seemed to be observant, understanding and appreciative.

Could you comment on that dream?

The Echo:
Hmn. Indeed. Understand within the unconscious, the subconscious of self, thee have, as it were, allowed without judgment that of the entering fully of that refer… (spirit guide.)

Author:
Wooowww.

(Laughing)

OK.

The Echo:
Understand it be presented to thee in symbolic format, merely for thy understanding. That of the winds that move the hair of the entity, Linda, be an visual presentation that the energy of Rogue be drawing directly toward thee with purpose and assurance of connection, you understand.

Client:
OK. That's interesting.

Another dream.
Friday overnight – Saturday morning June 24-25/05

A black boy was knocking things over in a store. Causing commotion. His mother was there. I had an idea that he was troubled. His mother told me that he had lost his father when he was small. She said he had...I'm not sure of my written words ...maybe anger or pain. I bent down and hugged him. I comforted him. It seemed like several minutes. It seemed to help him. I stood up. His mother came over. I put my hand on her shoulder and might have said something to her.

The Echo:
Hmn. Indeed. This be a presentation from thy subconscious of thy feelings of need to offer understanding, healings and love to all those about thee. That of the small black child be, here, reminiscent to we of that of the powers of negativity, that thee in sending love, peace and understanding can easily surmount. Speaking to mother is the presentation of the understandings to all of those about thee and it be then the choice of others to accept or reject those understandings.

Client:
There is another interesting dream. I have a long description. Cut me off at any point.

(Laughing)

Thursday-Friday Feb 24-25/05

Someone had moved in to a large, old house. I saw some women there. It seemed that they had to attend to something about the house. Seemed a little unsettled...disorganization. I was with some persons touring house. Huge inside compared to outside. I not tell anyone that I thought maybe the house was haunted.
Next, I was outside alone and I went inside through the side door. There was a loud bang on the wall at my left. I thought I would make a note about the noise and leave. I turned around and walked slowly through the outer room because I was not able to move my legs faster. I went outside. I returned with several persons (maybe all men). We were investigating. We

heard footsteps. I sensed that someone was following the sound in a room around a wall in front of us.

I turned right, into another room with two other persons. I heard steps and saw a woman in a high head-covering, like a medieval head-covering, and long dress, walk in front of me to the right and disappear through the wall. I was really impressed. She reappeared several feet to the left of the wall cradling a bundle in her arms, at a slight angle above horizontal. I thought perhaps flowers but it seemed to become long, lit candles. She seemed quite happy and quite pleasant. She walked away to our left and was looking back as if to see whether we were watching her. I waved to her and she waved back and disappeared. I was impressed. I thought this is my first apparition. Could you tell me about that dream?

The Echo:
Hmn. Indeed. Here the entity have been awarded, as it were, the opportunity of the actual viewing of…that of those in existence within that of other, or parallel realms. That of the spirit realm and the entity in its viewing be disengaged of its physical body and move to actual close resonance of the actions here described. The entity, in its waving to the spirit, be viewed by the spirit as another, because the entity be in, here refer, out-of-body resonance. The entity find high degree of reality within the remembrances of this occurrence and this be due to its out-of-body resonance in this instance. This be not in reality, be that refer dream, you understand. This be an viewing through an altered state of the entity's entire being.

Client:

(Laughing)

I don't know what's happening, but it is fun.

OK. Now here I think is a lucid dream. I don't know the symbolism in this one.

Thursday February 3/05   8:30 - 9 am

I had been up out of bed for a while and I just lay down on the bed for a short time. I have written lucid dream with a question mark. I was resting and my eyes were closed. I started meditating and visualizing. I was aware of mental images. Then I seemed to be with someone else on my right. I was vaguely aware that I was lying in bed and not wanting to fall asleep because I wanted to get up and do things shortly.

Not sure if we were in bodies. We might have been presences. It seemed like a bright kitchen. We were looking out a large, bright window. I saw a bright reddish-orange fox approaching out of a field carrying in its mouth a bright orange and white cat, probably dead, but the scene was not gory or violent. I hoped the cat was not actually hurt or dead. The fox put the cat down beside the road. An accompanying larger, dark gray or black bobcat picked it up. The two turned to my left along the road, trotting in step, lifting their legs high. I was impressed by the clarity, and brilliant colors and by two animals acting in unison and lifting their legs noticeably high. The scene seemed to be staged to hold my attention and maybe give me a message. Then I awoke to answer the ringing telephone.

The Echo:
Hmn. Indeed. These entities, here refer fox, bobcat, these entities be presented to thee…oh much as that of the North American natives refer thy animal totems, protectors, that be offered to thee visually. A fox for its craftiness, slyness of character and its determined will. The bobcat for its rapid movement, its skill at obtaining that which it desire and its strong ability of perception of all that is occurring about it.
This be presented to thee through thy own subconscious format to show thee that thy perceptions, thy ability of perception have dramatically increased and thee now have the ability to use this perception to aid others such as in the, here refer, dream format. The fox awarding the bobcat that of the prize of the orange cat, you understand, it be that of the awarding of thy own mind to give thy own mind the permission to be highly receptive and highly perceptive, at once and the same time, using thy thought patterns in a clever and reliable method, you understand.

Client:
You say that these animals are offered as totems and protectors. What would I do about it now? What would I do in a practical sense if I accept these qualities?

The Echo:
Indeed. The entity will learn slyness, the time to speak, the time to listen. The entity will also learn that of the doggedness of approach to others in order to obtain that which it desire. The, oh here refer, astuteness of the bobcat...here the entity will begin to see beyond the surface. The entity will begin to see within others in order to understand the reality of occurrences, rather than the mere, oh, shell of presentation from others. The entity will view deep within the souls of others in order to further understand them.

Client:
I have one more question. I do not recall the order of these two dreams. Often one dream will lead into another so I will give both dreams to you.

Sunday night – Monday morning September 5-6/04

I do not recall whether this is the first or second dream. A young Italian man said something to me. I asked him do I look like someone who has suffered? He looked into my eyes. I sensed he could see my past. He said yes.

Could you tell me about that dream?

The Echo:
Indeed. Here the entity be requesting permission from others to express the truth that lies within it. And in asking another to look into the eyes to see the suffering is akin to stating the truths that be known to thee with a degree of trepidation related to the acceptance of others. This be merely a presentation from the subconscious of self. And the entity in viewing this format have, in thy terms, lost the sense of trepidation. The acceptance of others, while important to thee, is not important to the point of

withholding from within.

Client:
Why was it a young Italian man?

The Echo:
Indeed it be merely that this entity be, that here referred, emissary of the, uh, that refer, pope, you understand. Within the understanding of the subconsciousness of the entity to gain acceptance from, that refer, pope is indeed difficult. Yet from the emissary of the pope is the same result with less difficulty.

Client:
This is the other dream from the same night.

I have written that I know the history of certain animals in the dream. There was a young bear, a wolf, a dog, and others with sharp teeth. Sometimes they seemed to challenge other persons or me or they would touch their teeth against someone else's hand or forearm or against mine. They would gently close their jaws to exert a slight pressure. I was annoyed that no one was there to control the animals. The touch of the teeth was uncomfortable, but not quite painful. I thought that I may have to do something to stop the animals. I knew that I would act if I became angry enough.

The Echo:
Indeed. The entity while it have, in colloquial terms, many entities nibbling at it, it indeed rise above through sheer determine of will. There be not fear of those that be nibbling at it and that it indeed maintain positivity and absolute control of its environs. It be once more a presentation from thy subconscious presented in symbolic format for thee to digest consciously.

Linda:
I had a recurring bad dream between the ages of eight and 10. I was afraid to go anywhere near a sofa and a chair in the living room, as if there were evil people who would grab me and pull me under, if I went too close. Could you tell me why I had this

dream?

The Echo:
Indeed. This be that of the remembrance format of the entity in its child mind of its prior incarnational experiences, as it be set upon by, here refer, oh, hidden aggrievors, understand. The entity have experienced an number of prior life formats that have come to an sudden demise due to entities emerging from hiding and striking thee physically. This be presented as an somewhat cleansing format of the memories, for the entity in its dream format have chosen to avoid and in the avoidance have released the negativity from within its being, you understand.

February, 2006
St. Catharines, Ontario

Present: Cliff Preston, channeling The Echo
          Linda Preston, directing the session
          Client

Client:
OK. Some dreams.

Tuesday, January 13, 2000 or before.

I was getting ready to carry the arm-piece of a cross. There were fittings for my arms. It might have been a procession. I was preparing or I had just started out. I felt chosen. There was no unhappiness.

The Echo:
This be a remembrance of the entity in, refer, celebration here within that of the land...oh in thy terms, refer, Greece. Here the entity be of high degree of adherence to, that refer, the Christian religion and the entity be in the celebration of, that refer, the crucifixion of Christ It be, as it were, chosen to impersonate that of the form of Jesus, Hesu. That it be highly receptive to

this. Be proud to be chosen to be the leading figure in the re-enactment of the crucifixion of Christ for this is an, here refer, high point of the Christian religious celebration format.

Client:
You are saying this that was the remembrance of an actual past life?

The Echo:
Indeed so.

Client:
Could you tell me roughly what year that would be?

The Echo:
Indeed it be of approximate year 1670 in thy present calendar usage.

Linda:
Was he an actor then?

The Echo:
Indeed not. As opposed to, that refer, actor, it be an zealot, you understand.

Client:
OK. I have another dream.

Tuesday-Wednesday, January 13-14, 2004.

I was at a Russian official hearing or trial. I placed some items beside a table leg at the front facing the assembly. I told two persons including Schevardnaze...and this is a direct quote that I remember: "In a Russian trial there are two prosecutors and no defence lawyers."

I thought that this was a clever comment to make and I thought that it would not be taken the wrong way and get me into trouble. Could you comment on that dream?

The Echo:
Hmm Indeed. Uh the entity be, that refer, insurgent, you understand, and this entity have been brought to trial as an enemy of the state and have indeed stated clearly that there indeed be two prosecutors for that of its, oh here refer, supposed defence lawyer is indeed an employee of the state and this be the, here refer, tongue-in-cheek statement of which the entity enter before the judges and leaders of the country. That of the items the entity place upon table...these be decided by the entity to be used as proof of innocence and these be ignored totally by, that refer, court. Therefore the entity be of high degree sardonic wit and cynicism knowing that its fate is sealed before trial as the trial be a sham, you understand.

Client:
In this dream I had no nervousness or no sense of unpleasantness and I was pleased with the comment that I made. Would this be a past life?

The Echo:
Indeed so. It be viewed strongly as that of prior existence format. The entity have taken that of, ah here refer, strong political stance within its existence and have entered into opposition of the cruel government policies and this be of approximate years... oh...oh approximate years of 1890 and it be...eh perhaps through to that of 1902 the entity be involved in acts in opposition to, that refer, czarist regime. Do not feel any compassion toward the czarist regime and feel not of concern for its own being for the entity feel that even death is preferable to existence within an oppressive state.

Client:
It is interesting that I would put a modern interpretation on this dream. Schevardnaze is a modern political figure.

The Echo:

Indeed so. This be merely due to the subconscious of self in knowing of this entity, you understand, and therefore it be placed before thee that of the face of authority.

Client:
One more dream.
Tuesday-Wednesday April 19-20 2005

I have written driver touted his small sporty car, possibility a convertible. I started as a passenger in the front seat, but then somehow I was in the back. He drove the car up steep high hills. We were presences rather than bodies. I thought cars are wonderful but roads on hills should not be so steep. I have written that the car almost flew. The road seemed like almost a 90-degree angle and I wondered who would put a road on such a steep hill. I had some fear that the car would fall off the hill, but in this dream, and in similar dreams, the car always reaches the top. Could you explain this?

The Echo:
Indeed. This be that of message to self from…uh…subconscious self, to show to thee that are no barriers in thy existence. That thee can move ahead regardless of what others place before thee. That even do the, oh here refer, walls be straight up and down, thee have the ability to climb the mountains with confidence or to circumnavigate the barrier, as it were. That this be strong availability to thee. Thee have only to accept that there are no barriers you understand.

Chapter 10   Meditation – Automatic writing

The following are   excerpts from transcripts of personal automatic writing sessions, during meditations, by a person who practiced meditation with Cliff and Linda Preston and developed the capacity for automatic writing through the former discipline. The purpose of meditation is to achieve relaxation, inner peace, self-awareness and direct contact with God. Beyond that, it is a personal choice to ask conscious questions and receive answers.   Permission was obtained to publish this excerpt, keeping the identity confidential.

Thursday,   June26/03

Question:
Message for today.

Answer:
God. More than ever. Here. Summer. Energy high. Opening to understanding. Finding inner peace, strength. Help is always available. Life sometimes difficult because all is in your mind. Positive and negative. Negative (*word unclear*) remains with you because you create and recreate it. You don't need it. Stay in spirit, in positive to be positive. Constantly check self, remind if necessary, stay in positive. You can do it. You are doing it. Energy, enthusiasm increase. Believe in power of self. Take control of self. Keep a world in your mind. Make your world. Create. Do. Think. Act. Be positive. Create positive world rather than merely trying to avoid negative. Remember you are doing well in difficult circumstances. Remember you can

remove/reduce difficult circumstances at will. You are learning.

Tuesday, July 1/03

Sense a presence to my left, energy patterns flash on and off in visualizations, brief ringing left ear.

Wednesday, July 2/03

Question:
What best way for me to use my time this summer?

Answer.
Opening to spirit. To possibilities. Thinking in new ways. Doing things. Organizing house and all endeavors. Apply rising energy. Helping others such as (persons named).

Tuesday, July 8/03

Question:
How do I fulfill my life purpose?
How do I stay joyful with problems?

Answer:
You are fulfilling.
Constant work. Rededicate life to spirit regularly. Shift awareness to spirit from physical realm. Problems will seem smaller, manageable. Will go away. You will see life differently. You have a problem only if you think you have. Life can be difficult. We acknowledge this. But not as difficult if you keep awareness in spirit. You can always enjoy many things in life even if not all things seem perfect to you. Bring concerns to spirit. Acknowledge them and leave them. We wish you the joy of spirit. We wish you to see that you are spirit. You are not a failure because some difficulties have been given to you. Do not judge yourself. Realize that you are wonderful. You are spirit. You are always with God. Your 'human life of difficulties' is short. You do not see your life as difficult. Only occasionally you get discouraged. Understandable. We send you love and

strength. You always come back with renewed purpose. You will experience many more good things. Your life in transition. You are handling well, otherwise this life, these circumstances would not have been chosen for you. Your enthusiasm is returning. We commend you.

Wednesday, July 9/03

Question:
Message for today.

Answer:
Be the person you want to be. You are now. Tell yourself you are. You control who you are, your thoughts, actions. Ideas coming to you. Look at everything in your life. Decide want it or not.

Question:
Why is automatic writing comparatively difficult today?

Answer:
Sleepiness. Tranquility now. May be best for you now. May not need more information now. Direct replenishment, contact from within. Infuse soul with love, understanding. Feeling this now is perhaps better than automatic writing today.

Question:
Now automatic writing seems better. There are feelings with the information.

Answer:
Some contradictions perhaps. Feelings, changes. Automatic writing leads to answers. Much emotion recently. Negative. Difficult to work through. Difficult time, we acknowledge. You are moving ahead. Testing. Trials. Rest needed. Acceptance. See from a high perspective. Do not worry daily things. Clear mind.

Thursday, July 10/03

Question:
Please say something new. My spiritual progress. Life in general.

Answer:
Your daily routine may be spiritual. Keep right attitude of making a contribution in everything you do. Large and small things. You do not have to progress materially. Only spiritually. You have been chosen for a certain purpose. You can do it. All you have to do is keep right attitude. Everything will follow. You will make progress. Relax. No timetable. Accept life as it comes when you have right attitude of service to God and others. This life is temporary and illusory. You are in spirit. You will understand after you shift your consciousness fully back to spirit from material world. You may think physical was a deception. Unnecessary. You will be glad to be home in spirit. You will understand then. Nothing can hurt your essence. Buddhism says let go of illusion to reach spirit. This appeals to you. You may use some Buddhist ideas for your spiritual growth. Good to want to give some of your unneeded possessions to others but most important just to be free of distractions, weights holding you down in material world. You can free your spirit more and more. May not always be easy, but worth doing. It is the only way, best way for you. Stay open to your higher self and to spirit.

Tuesday, July 15/03
Peaceful. Automatic thinking (thoughts not written), guidance to me. Be in spirit, love, acceptance, peace of mind

Wednesday, July 16/03
Deep peace. Self instruction, floating on clouds as spirit.
Review something good from every year of my life. Send God's love and blessing.

Monday, July 21/03
Asked help me remember three dreams from overnight - one remembered immediately

Wednesday, July 23/03

Question:
Message for today for me.

Answer:
Simplify life, strengthen who you are. Spend more time on important things. Organize your life. Categorize. "Take stock." Make decisions what you want and work for it. Get rid of other things, objects from house, objects from mind, be open, be aware of possibilities. Have faith. Life is good. Make your life good. Manage problems. Stay above problems. Life can seem difficult at times but you can stay above difficulties by your attitude and what you give attention to. Live in spirit and you will be part of something greater than a single life, you will be life, you will be spirit. It takes work. It is a life's work. Every day is a new life. Precious. Full of opportunity. You are reborn each day. You can be who you want to be. Do not live in past. Live in present opportunity. You co-create your reality with God. Believe this and you can do it. Live one day at a time. Patience. Accomplish each day and imagine even more accomplishments, if you did not actually finish all you wanted to do.

Sometimes imagination is the precursor to reality. Believe in self, believe that God has given you the opportunity to do all that you want to do.

Monday, July 28/03

Question:
Comment on trips to (named).

Answer:
Important. One contact with spirit. Inspiring. Opens an individual's mind to possibilities. Greatness of life. Some experience of the "other side" on Earth . Keep going. Balance. Anchor in life. Safe journeys.

Wednesday, August 6/03

Question:
Are you there with me?

Answer:
Yes, always. You don't always know it, but it is not difficult to be aware of us. You have learned. You must now stay in control of your life, your mind, your energy. Bring what you want into your life. Time is right now. Begin new projects. Make your meditation tapes etc. Follow spiritual path. You will do well. You believe. You must make effort by deciding to stay in spirit more. You are succeeding. We ask that you rededicate yourself to spirit. Review what you have learned. You can develop more enthusiasm. Your energy cycle is increasing, moving to the top. You will have several good months. Believe. Believe. Believe. You can create the conditions and circumstances that you want.

Friday, August 8/03
Question:
What are best things to do today?

Answer:
Think new thoughts. Be in spirit. Open mind. Eliminate clutter mental and physical. Give things away. Find God and self. Travel. Experience. Do for others and self. Feel love. Feel joy. Send love and joy. Relax. Enjoy life. Life is what you think, say and do. Others do not make your life. You make your own life. Relax. Keep mind free of worry. Create positive energy by thought, by will.

Question:
Please advise re my career.

Answer:
Continue on present path. As you work and develop, ideas will come. Your actions, thoughts will determine the course you take.

Tuesday, August 12/03
Question:
How may I accomplish things?

Answer:
Read your notes regularly. Practice what you learn. Stay in spirit. You are chosen. It may be difficult but worth it. Believe in self. Have one or two main pursuits in your life. Work accordingly on them. Simplify. Remove distractions. Build your spirit. Approach your life with a spiritual attitude. You are learning that there is a lot more (and less) to life than you had thought. Trust in self and spirit. Strengthen thinking. Consider what can do for career/income. Work toward it. Best plan is to work for spiritual purpose.

Question:
How can I find strength and self control?

Answer:
Progress. Talk to God. Talk to Spirit. Your approaches to God have always been welcomed. Live one day at a time. Do not blame self. Learn from circumstances, especially difficult circumstances. You are doing it for God. We are aware of it. Enjoy your life. You do mostly. Remember that all difficulties pass.

Wednesday, August 20/03
Question:
How close to a spiritual breakthrough?

Answer:
You are breaking through every day. Every realization of God's love is a breakthrough from daily living in world with mentality of world. Believing that there is much more is a breakthrough. If you forget, lose the feeling of spirit, it is a breakthrough to regain idea and feeling. You can live in spirit. It changes your life and lives of those you touch. If you keep in spirit always, you can always do the work of spirit. Special things happen, outside of and above your everyday living. Believe in spirit, trust in spirit, desire to do spirit works are necessary. That is all that is necessary.

Question:
Name one wonderful thing that is going to happen.

Answer:
Every new day is wonderful. You are alive. You have more opportunities to do good, accomplish, be happy, develop insight. Be in spirit. Reach your goals, set new goals. Highest order be interested, seek, delight in knowledge, go beyond each time you learn, accomplish something. Add to the total of knowledge and to the total of experience, to the total of love, and of accomplishment. Move forward. There is no failure. Expand. Improve. Think well of self and others. Experience happiness. Fulfillment.

Friday, August 22/03

Question:
Talk about computers relating to me.

Answer:
Learn more. You have career. You understand, appreciate computers. Fascinated by technology. Continue. Pursue career. Learn possibilities re your computers. Get most from. How to fix, solve problems. You can do it. Keep records, notes. You will enjoy more. You will feel control, understanding. Organized. You will find God in (*the pleasure of the productive use of*) computers, as you have. (*On one occasion that you were particularly pleased*) You said "God is everything" and touched your computers and printers. It is true. You are discovering truths.

Friday, September 5/03

Question:
Tell me about manifesting as in Wayne Dyer book.

Answer:
You attract what you want that serves a higher purpose and you are able to receive it by love and belief or awareness. May be

attitudes of mind, conditions in life, physical things etc. They already exist. You can bring them to you by proper attitude and desire. These may represent your attitude. An outer representation of your inner, unseen self, your spirit. Love is everything as the book says. Practice being in spirit, in unconditional love. You will be able to continue for longer periods. Living as unconditional love is highest goal. Some have attained this. This is full, conscious union with God. This is a worthwhile life pursuit.

Friday, September 12/03
Peaceful, feeling of miracles, want to share peace of mind, joy, love, wisdom, awareness, miracles

Question:
What did it mean when I won a draw at the computer club?

Answer:
You are enthusiastic. You enjoy computers. You have drawn the prize to yourself. You are aware that you do this. Means also that you can create good in your life. Good for self and others. Specifically, you can see possibilities from winning this prize. You consider choices. You can decide what to do. Ideal is to continue enthusiasm, do more, accomplish more, enjoy yourself. Expand your awareness of self, life, others, computers. Dream. Make a choice, act upon choice. Prizes stimulate thoughts, dreams, feelings, excitement. Your spirit becomes larger. No obligation or set course for prize-winning. But certainly to get your attention, create feelings, mental conditions that lead to more things.

Thurs September 18/03

Question:
Please comment on "God is everything."

Answer:
You have felt this. Feeling becomes knowing. You have been

able to stay in this feeling/knowing condition for periods of time. If you want, you are staying in condition longer. This is living in spirit. The easiest way for you to live. All is peace and love. There is no discord, as in your realm, Earth. You can live this way on Earth. Imagine improving relations with all those in your life. Can be done. You can not control others or make them into something better if they do not choose, but you can lead goodness out of them, lead them to goodness. Certainly you can control how you act about them and think about them. You control how you act and think at all times. Put discord out of your life. You can understand that all events are for a purpose, good or bad events. Ultimately, there are no bad events as all can join God and all can have peace, love and understanding. All are safe from Earth's discord, what can then be seen as an illusion, a creation of human minds on Earth. Often a struggle to do good on Earth, but worth it. This is life purpose. DO GOOD. Simply that. Difficult and easy. Right frame of mind, open, loving heart make it easy. Yes, God is everything. Trust God always. Keep God in your heart and mind and stay in God, as a perfecting, experiencing part of God. You are receiving peace as you write this. It is fulfilling, complete peace. Stay in God in your thoughts, attitudes, actions. Love. You can create mountains of love, of achievement, of good. Then as you pass to the next world, you will have a short, easy trip from the mountain you have created. This is enough for now. Keep this message in your heart. You may return to your routine now.

Monday, September 22/03

Question:
Message for today.

Answer:
Difficult but worth living in spirit. Help available. Guidance, Strength. Love. You have a cheering section. You (*all human beings*) are special. Courage, dedication, love required to live a human life. Remember that you are spirit, keep a higher perspective and all is well. Your thoughts and emotions are important because as you think, you experience. Think as spirit

and experience as spirit, with love, with communion with all others and God. You are joined to everything. You are part of the whole. Live with love, peace, acceptance. Always be calm. This means clarity of vision, of thought. Stay connected. Do not cut yourself off. You can connect with everyone you encounter. Instead, often human beings appear others, (*words unclear*), dismiss. You are thus isolating yourself from others and yourself. Approach with openness. All else follows.

Tuesday, October 14/03

Question:
Message for today?

Answer:
You have been away from your practice of meditation, automatic writing and channeling. You are able to do it regularly, and other things in your life. Put your well-being first. Then you will be able to help others. Only you can take care of yourself, as God intended. You need not let other things cause you to abandon your schedule. You need some time for yourself regularly. Especially for the spiritual side.

Question:
How do I deal with anger, frustration, impatience?

Answer:
You are dealing with these things. By wanting to do better, by knowing you can, by living in spirit at all times, within and without. You are spirit. Things of the spirit are peace, love, calm, joy, understanding. You will not consider negativity when you are in spirit. It will not exist.

Question:
Send a message of Joy.

Answer:
You are alive. Infinite possibilities. Live in spirit. Program self to enjoy life, be happy, not worry about negative. You are fine,

safe. Your spirit is growing. This world will not hurt you. It is only a journey

Monday, October 27/03
Smell of smoke

Question:
Is there a new message?

Answer:
You can write with your eyes closed. You can stay on the lines. We will guide you. Practice everything spiritual. It all has meaning, a purpose. Be all that you are. Practice your work. Open your mind completely. Accept spirit. This is your life. You will be taken care of, provided for. Do not worry about money or regular material living. You are meant for something else. You know this is true. Trust the feeling and ideas that come to you. We send them. You are rising to another level. Keep going. The smoke smell is one sign for you. Do you think of Joan of Arc? What do you think? Is there smoke in your eyes? What do you need to continue your work? You can accept all that you ... We can provide it. Think more about manifesting. You can do it. Act now. Unfetter yourself.

Wednesday, November 5/03

Question:
Message for today.

Answer:
Stay in spirit so that all things are possible. Your dreams exist in spirit. All that is good exists in spirit. You are free in spirit to love, create, help, glorify goodness and God. You are what you think, say and do. So you can be anything that you want to be. You are creating yourself and your world with each thought. It takes effort, but being in spirit is a natural state after you release negativity. Not only does negativity not have any value, it hurts you, lessens you. Why not freely give it up? Then you have everything - your freedom, love, peace - all creation, existence.

You are a part of this. Keep your mind on this. It is wonderful. It is everything. Do not use your mind to hurt self or others, or to diminish or lessen your world or self or others. Create. Build. Love. Exist in its highest form. This is everything. This is God.

Wednesday, November 12/03
Interested but tired, lack purpose and energy

Question:
Message for today.

Answer:
As always. Be aware of higher things. This is your true life. You can create Heaven on Earth . You will have everything you want and need. If you do not have it, it is not important to you. Be who you are. Who you can be, that you have not been. You can always do something, improve yourself and your world. No matter what obstacles. You control your mind. The most powerful object in your life. Use it well. Use it to create the world you want.

Question:
Why does my attitude/outlook rise and fall. Why assured sometimes, but uneasy other times?

Answer:
You do this by neglect, lack of care. Your consciousness is precious. Guard it. You have heard that you can not afford a negative thought. Why would you want a negative thought? Why put negativity into your world? You are the creator. Learn to create only spirit, only positive. Keep the ability. Live in the ability. Negative times, thoughts will lessen and even become extinct. You control your mind.

Tuesday, November 18/03
Calm, sense of purpose

Message - Simplify. Remove clutter. Organize. Review notes. You are on right track. Important to spend more time on the few most important things in your life. Spirituality/channeling, computers, planning, relationships, helping others. You can keep in proper frame of mind by listening to direction, believing in self and message, knowing that you will succeed. You are doing well. Do not have to worry about every dollar. Move ahead. Accept the things you are ready for. You have prepared well. Important things to do. You are chosen for specific reasons. You are the one for your plan. Believe in self and in us and in message. Keep joy in heart. Then all will be well. See the big, bigger picture. You decide what to make of each moment of your life. Decide well for Heaven on Earth . You know that you can do it. We know it too. You have been chosen for your plan. You have chosen it yourself. Live every minute of every day. You will succeed.

Friday, November 27/03

Question:
Go to computer show? (*A long way in bad weather.*)

Answer:
You have the spirit. Need not go. Can get as much or more enjoyment, learning, from using computer at home. It is always what you bring to something that makes it what it is for you. You are the main element. External things can be good in themselves. You make them better. Your decision, as always, what to do. We can offer what we know as information for you to use.

Monday,   December 8/03

Answer:
Take stock. Review. Organize. Plan. Act. Time is near for great things. Believe in heart and soul. Live your belief. The masters do this. You are an initiate. You have distance to go. You are receiving help. No one walks alone. You are gathering the positive energies you need. Rest, reflect often when you get too much into physical world and not enough in spirit world. You are free spirit. This is your course, your path. This is also the path for all. You are among those who have heeded this call.

Have decided on the course of spirit. You will be rewarded as you go along. In different ways. Believe, stand aside and let your higher self, spirit guide you. At this time of year take care of self and others. You are all that some have. They are all that you have. Everything works if people allow it. Simple and difficult. Keep doing your part, more. Others will do theirs. Create your own special world. Invite others to share it. Some will be like-minded. You are moving forward. You can do great things as all can. Return to spirit as often as necessary. Spirit is everything.

Thursday, December 11/03

The (*project named*). Time is right. This has been a reality in our world. We can create it instantaneously. You are able to manifest in your world what has been first created in our world. You like to think of it in a fanciful mood but you will have to think of it in a practical mood. Big job. Worth doing. Can lead to more good things. Will be (*successful*) because it is needed. Direct good created, and spin off, ripple effect. It can have life of its own. You need only believe to be able to do it. Belief plus desire equals doing, completion. Wonderful experience. We encourage you and the others to do this (*project*). You are well suited for this work. We encourage you. You are learning about manifesting and co-creating good. This project is next step for you. We will help you learn what is necessary for completion. Work is being done at other end to set stage. Remember. Belief. Belief. Belief. Then you will be able to do.

Monday, January 5/04

Question:
Please tell me about living in spirit.

Answer:
You are. You do. Be aware of it to accomplish it properly You are on right track. By wanting to do it, you are. Program yourself for love and peace, not frustration or anger. Also, consciously think before you do something, such as say

something to another. Think even before you think. Thoughts are under your control. The building blocks of reality. You control your own thoughts. Do not give away control. Do not speculate what others may be thinking. You are responsible only for your own thoughts. You can create a world of love and peace. This is your world. See how you are part of God, part of spirit. You can create as spirit does. You are always learning and improving. Keep moving ahead. Same attitude in all things. You can free yourself, strengthen yourself, love yourself in your thoughts. Then you will have everything you need. Ask God or spirit only for the ability to make your own world of good. This another way of asking God for help but this way you can see that you are in control. When in control, you feel love, joy, gratitude, what you are meant to understand. You can stay in spirit consciously and return consciously when you leave it, but you are always in spirit even if unknown to your consciousness. There may be different ways of expressing well-known truths that have always been known but have to be learned and relearned by every human being. If you want to live in spirit and make the effort, you will truly live in spirit. This is full life. There is no other life.

Question:
Please inform about (*project named*).

Answer:
The time has come for the (*project named*), as you know. This will give you more sense of purpose. It will continue you on the right path. More things will open to you and for those in the (*project*). It will spread their message. Another voice for them. Good undertaking for all involved.

Question:
Why do I sometimes want to return to daily activity when I meditate?

Answer:
Restless. Impatient. Looking in daily routine for meaning, for importance of life, but this is a habit. You are entering

consciously spirit more and more. You will choose spirit and become accustomed to it. You have always been strongly attached in a good way to your life, which is often daily routine. You want to do it well, understand it. But there is much more to life or much more beyond your life, as you have been learning. Just keep making effort to be in spirit more and you will be in spirit. Keep going.

Wednesday, January 7/04

Question:
How find peace, calm mood?

Answer:
You are doing now. By addressing a problem. Acknowledging it. Know you are stronger. Know you are above it. You are much more than a thought or a feeling. Refuse to be negative or to have negative thoughts. Replace with truth about who you are, power of your mind and heart to live as spirit. Difficulties are challenges to overcome. You can make them larger or shrink and eliminate problems. It is how you look at things. How you know things, know your reality. Return to spirit 100 times a day if necessary. You are in physical world. There are challenges, opportunities for you to handle well and grow. Realize you are also in spirit where nothing negative exists unless you create it for self and fool self into thinking it is real and permanent. If you don't think of something, it does not exist. If you think of it, you create it and recreate it. Stop. Be peaceful. Allow spirit to come to you, be your guide. You can have knowledge that you are doing well, you are safe, held in love, nothing can hurt you, your essence, your spirit. Remember there is always some good in everything or, specifically, in your reaction to it. Always look for good way of handling problem. Learn. Report lesson to spirit and you will realize that you are part of a whole. You are accepted, recognized, understood. You are not alone. This knowledge will always give you strength. You have said physical life is a temporary illusion. Don't get upset by things in it. Look beyond individual existence on Earth to vast universe, to spirit, to reality. We love you. You love us and all of spirit. That

is known, that is reality. Move ahead through learning, loving, consolidating your identity, your knowledge, put pieces of puzzle together. You will complete puzzle with head and heart. By helping others, you help self. By giving to God, you receive from God. Review what you have learned and experienced over the last several years. It will help you in difficult times and add to your flights of joy in good times. This knowledge and love will connect you more closely to all, to spirit, to universal life.

Tuesday, January 13/04

Question:
When I feel anger and anxiety in the air, where does it come from?

Answer:
Many sources. Like attracting like. You are sensitive. Increasingly. You can feel the upset. For the anger, the mood… "misery loves company." It wants to infect others. Best defense is what you do already. Realize. Pause. Invoke spirit to surround you. Realize your will is strong. Nothing can hurt you. It will dissipate in face of spirit, in light of spirit.

Chapter 11   Code of Living and Other Statements

The Echo's Code of Living presented during a deep-trance channeling session of The Echo by Cliff Preston in 1983. Cliff and Linda Preston have since followed this ethic in their daily lives.

Make every effort to see problems from both your viewpoint and the viewpoint of others.

Harm no one, physically, mentally, emotionally, or spiritually.

Do not cause others to experience guilt or fear.

Do cause others to experience love and trust of you.

Remove judgmentalism from your thought processes.

Remember the Universal Law of Karma: You will reap what you sow.

Offer assistance and understand, if it is turned down, that each entity has total free choice in its life.

The only crime is to force another to any action or thought against its will.

View all beings as spirits and you will begin to see the beauty of them all.

Treat no one in any manner that you could not or would not accept for self.

Other Statements by The Echo

Those entities that think they can, can.
Those entities that think they can't, are completely correct.
(1980)

Belief is that which you have been taught and have accepted as truth.
Truth is that which you have personally experienced and examined. (1983)

Love is the only answer, regardless the question. (1985)

To blindly follow the belief of another is to accept the totality of mental and emotional slavery. (1987)

Crossing Over:
Please remember, that no one is ever really lost.
Crossing over is just another part of the human experience and for most it is a welcome change. The person is birthing into the Spiritual Realm and someday soon, when it chooses, will birth again into the Physical Realm.
So it continues for each of us until we have finally learned all we feel we need to learn and can then return to our Godhead.
Only those left behind mourn for the lost one, and in fact, the mourning is most often for self, not for the loved one.
Rather than mourn or fret at the passing of your loved one, celebrate that you have associated with her/him and have contributed in some manner, yet unknown to you, to the enrichment of her/his experience.
Send them on with Love and the knowledge that, if you wish, you may meet again, at another time and another place, to continue helping each other in your travels through experience and time. (2002)

Go in peace. Go in love and understanding. (For many years, the final message of   The Echo at every deep-trance channeling session by Cliff Preston.)
Echo Monthly Session – Closing Comments, February 4, 2004

Present: Cliff and Linda Preston
  Three clients learning channeling.

The Echo:
We would say to each and every entity present, that there be here an strong grouping of individuals. That the spiritual responses of each of these entities be strong, indeed, and yet be developing comparative stronger, each and every day.

The entities present be nearly of one mind, in that each entity have strong desires to assist those about them to the utmost of abilities. This be highly commendable, and we say to these entities present, merely be in full awareness of thy abilities.

It be not necessary to maintain abilities the same as another individual. For all individuals are unique and separate. Therefore, develop those abilities for which thee feel comfortable in using. Be not in attempt to perform in an particular set of rules. For, understand, in the dealing of spiritual energies, in the dealing of healings offered to others, there can be no rules. There are only individual responses.

Trance Practice Friday May 14, 2004

Present: Cliff and Linda Preston
  Three clients learning channeling.

Q: Echo would you please comment on how those present this evening can remove negative self-judgmentalism.

Echo: This be a simple matter indeed. Don't.

Firstly be in awareness of why an entity enter into judgment of self. Firstly the entities tend to enter into a degree of comparative thought and we speak here in general terms. An entity that be in judgement of self is doing so because it has entered into comparative thought patterns and that it has accepted particular social understandings.

Be aware that most of thy social rulings are in fact false in relation to the reality of being. Therefore here, when an entity is in judgment of self, the entity may be asking self. Am I good enough as compared to something or someone else? Am I actually performing the trance state for I have been told all my life and socially accepted that this can not happen or that this must not happen?

Separate within thy mind the understanding of the reality of thy existence and the acceptance of thy social standards or thy judgment related to others. We do not speak of this in a wide scope. This may occur within minute detail within the mind of an entity.

For example, a woman must needs be sweet and kind and loving. Understand that this is not a woman, this is a social understanding of what a woman needs to present to the world in order to be judged acceptable by others about it. The reality of that particular woman may be that it do not wish to be kind and loving and understanding or neat in its clothing. The entity wish only to be its own person, its own being, regardless of the thoughts or acceptances of others.

An entity that be cast into the woods, for example, at an approximate age five of years and somehow find a means of existence, growing, developing, living in the woods for its entire existence - this entity goes through its entire existence without thoughts of comparison to others and without guilt in any form in its being. The entity only does that which the entity does and does not feel guilt of self-judgment.

Guilt, self-judgment, comparisons are all related to the social understandings in which thee develop and in which thee accept. Therefore, choose (repeat, choose) to accept particular social standards, social judgments, only after thee have entered a decision to do so. Do not accept social standards or social judgments merely by rote. This will then remove from self that refer self-judgment. It will set the soul free and the entities will no longer be afraid to voice the words or thoughts that be passing through their minds.

For each and every entity is aware, as they enter into practice within the trance state, there are many thoughts, many ideas, flowing through the mind at once and the same instance. The entities however tend to select that which may 'sound OK' to others. This again is a social judgment. This is the presentation of a social standard in order to gain acceptance from others in the social grouping. Rather, do there be words moving through thy mind, thoughts moving through thy mind, that in thy understanding thee fear may cause others to be somewhat socially shocked, somewhat repulsed, somewhat in disbelief – reject that and speak the words that need to be said, merely because they need to be said.

A number of years ago, Linda Preston wrote the following essay about a possible past and future of the human race, in a mood of hope and concern.

SCIENCE FICTION?

What if, 4 1/2 million years ago, we were an advanced people from another planet?
What if, we once were more intelligent?
What if, we once were more intuitive?
What if, we once were more telepathic?
What if, we once were more creative?
What if, we once were capable of teleporting?
What if, we once were loving and caring?
What if, we once used 90 % of our brain and, now, use only 2%?
What if, we came to this planet as a prison?
What if, we, then, destroyed our planet with global nuclear war?
What if, the only survivors were small groups of people scattered around the world who had descended into savagery?
What if, we, then, advanced to 'normal' and, again, destroyed our planet with global nuclear war?
What if, we did this more than 200 times and the last time was Atlantis?
What if, we, the peoples of Atlantis, became power-hungry and, still, had not learned the lessons of our history and destroyed ourselves again?
What if, at that time, we were an advanced people and had sent out spaceships to explore the universe?

What if, these spacemen set up a base on the other side of the moon, and effectively, occasionally, sent spaceships to check on the Earth to see if radioactive levels had decreased?

What if, there still remained a civilization on the other side of the moon?

What if, these "Extra-Terrestrials" are different in appearance than, Man, now, mutated because of more than 200 past nuclear wars or Earth changes?

What if, we are at a point of time, when we might have a nuclear war?

What if, we are now in the process of changing our atmosphere, and, 200 years in the future, we may be in the "starting over" process?

What if, this time, NONE survive?

WHAT IF?

Afterword

The Echo, and other spiritual teachers, say that there is no such thing as the "paranormal" because everything that exists in the universe is real and normal. They prefer the term "metaphysical" because it allows for the fact that the human mind may not be able to understand a manifestation of the spiritual realm, where we have the greater part of our existence, beyond this physical realm. With this point of view, we could approach unexplainable events with open minds, rather than with fear, ridicule or denial. We could not offer our ignorance or discomfort as proof that something could not exist.

A paradox of life is that although human beings are inseparable parts of a universal life energy, that some call God, we are convinced that we are separate and alone. If we believe in God, many of us think that he, she or it, is an unknowable, remote force that is nothing like us. There is no common ground and no possible way to encounter God until after we die. God is too important and too busy for us now. The best we can do is forward our prayers and hope that God agrees.

Why are we ready to accept this idea that God, who wants nothing to do with us until after we die, would have any interest in us at all? Would an introduction to this eternal being, while we are alive, not be a good way to prepare for our afterlife?

Some spiritual traditions teach that God is within us. We may achieve direct knowledge and direct experience of God by quieting our minds, putting aside our egos, and listening to our inner silence. We may then determine that we are from God, of God, and part of God. In fact, an inseparable part of God, who is always with us. This is the reason that God is interested in us and can have direct contact with us.

Is it not logical that one part of God can communicate with another part? Or communicate with all the parts, or complete essence at the same time? Perhaps there is nothing new to communicate since everything is already known. Perhaps we are receiving reminders of things that we have overlooked or forgotten. Perhaps when we know something or feel something intuitively, we are receiving a reminder from the spiritual realm. If this is true, then psychic mediums and channelers must be receiving reminders, tips, warnings, and insights that the spiritual realm wants us to have. Could this spiritual electronic mail system have been set up once, before time or outside of time, with the send message key always depressed, in order for us to stay in awareness?

It is said that in our higher selves we can know God, think like God. and even act like God. When we help another person, this is what God would do. When we send love for hate, this is what God would do. When we forgive, this is what God would do. God could do nothing else in these circumstances.

We say that God is love, or peace, or wisdom, and can be found in silence or stillness. Some spiritual teachers suggest that our minds can lead us away from God, if used incorrectly. The human mind creates the ego, the illusion of separateness from God. The ego gives us a false sense of identity. The ego insists to us that it is real and different from everyone else, often better than everyone else, and right when everyone else is wrong. It tells us that it wants what is best for us, but it separates us from other people and it can set us against them. Thus it separates us from God.

Some spiritual teachers suggest that we use our minds only when necessary, that we control our thinking and apply it only to such practical things as our work. The rest of the time we could turn off our minds and allow our inner silence, stillness, or awareness to expand. There we will discover who we really are. There we will also discover God. Are we listening to the silence?

Help is always available

If you want answers to your questions about life
or help with any problem, large or small,
Cliff and Linda Preston may be able to help.

A channeling session of The Echo can give you answers about various areas of your life such as
health and medical information, relationships, career and finances, and dream interpretation.

Hypnosis, tarot card readings, handwriting analysis, numerology and other disciplines can provide insight into your life and practical help with such things as stress management or overcoming negative thinking and unwanted habits.

Learn to do what Cliff and Linda do

Cliff and Linda offer courses in psychic and spiritual development such as self-awareness, meditation and automatic writing; and past-life workshops.

Learn more at   cpreston@becon.org

Order Form

To order copies of
Cliff Preston channels The Echo Book 1
Cliff Preston channels The Echo Book 2
Cliff Preston channels The Echo Book 3

please detach or photocopy this form, print clearly, and mail it with your cheque payable to

Cliff Preston
79 Burleigh Road North
Ridgeway ON Canada L0S 1N0

Send to:
Name _____

Address _____

Prov/State _____ Postal/Zip _____
Country _____
Email _____

Copy(s) at $24.95
    Book 1 _____
    Book 2 _____
    Book 3 _____
    Add delivery $4.00 Canada
             $5.00 U.S.

    Total Books _____ Total Amount _____

www.ingramcontent.com/pod-product-compliance
Lightning Source LLC
Chambersburg PA
CBHW071713160426
43195CB00012B/1669